12/14

	DATE DUE	
MAR 2 7 2019		

THE MILLIONAIRE MASTER PLAN

THE MILLIONAIRE MASTER PLAN

Your Personalized Path to Financial Success

ROGER JAMES HAMILTON

BUSINESS PLUS

NEW YORK   BOSTON

Business Plus
Hachette Book Group
237 Park Avenue
New York, NY 10017

www.HachetteBookGroup.com

Printed in the United States of America

RRD-C

First Edition: July 2014
10 9 8 7 6 5 4 3 2 1

Business Plus is an imprint of Grand Central Publishing.
The Business Plus name and logo are trademarks of Hachette Book Group, Inc.

The publisher is not responsible for websites (or their content) that are not owned by the publisher.

Library of Congress Cataloging-in-Publication Data

Hamilton, Roger James.
    The millionaire master plan : your personalized path to financial success / Roger James Hamilton. — First edition.
        pages cm
    Includes index.
    Summary: "The Millionaire Master Plan is a unique and fresh approach as to how individuals can not only get a sense of where they stand on the spectrum of personal wealth, but more importantly, how they can learn to ascend from their present state to a higher level. Roger James Hamilton, himself a highly successful entrepreneur and successful investor, has designed nine steps - from barely surviving - all the way to the highest level of ultimate wealth for life - and he lays out his nine steps in an easy-to-understand color-coded manner that ranges from red (barely living paycheck-to-paycheck) all the way to ultra-violet (where generating income is simply no longer a worry). Along the way, the reader first takes a quick test to determine where one is on the financial spectrum, and then Hamilton provides key insights and practical tips as to how one can progress to the next level. You track your progress by ascending from one color to the next"— Provided by publisher.
    ISBN 978-1-4555-4923-8 (hardback) — ISBN 978-1-4555-4924-5 (ebook) — ISBN 978-1-4789-5374-6 (audio download) 1. Finance, Personal. 2. Wealth. 3. Investments. 4. Success in business. I. Title.
    HG179.H2542 2014
    332.024'01—dc23

                                                                                2014002784

    ISBN (intl.): 978-1455-58399-7

Dedicated to Renate,
Kathleen, Theresa, and Luke.
You are my light.

CONTENTS

PART III

THE ENTERPRISE PRISM AND BEYOND

THE
MILLIONAIRE
MASTER
PLAN

GREETINGS FROM BALI

Hong Kong, Christmas 1988: I was nineteen years old, sitting with my parents, brother, and sister talking about where we wanted to be in thirty years. Strangely, we all fantasized about the same thing: owning a resort on a paradise island where we could spend time together and live in nature. We weren't wealthy and had no way to afford a resort, but we had spent my childhood on the beaches of Papua New Guinea, and they had been very happy years. Compared with Hong Kong—well, there was no comparison.

We all agreed it was a wonderful dream that Christmas Day, but that was all it was, and I went off to college to be an architect instead. I had made it to my fifth year in the seven-year program when I realized I still had decades to go before I would see the fruition of my training. I didn't want to wait until I was in my sixties to reap the rewards of my work! I thought about my dream of one day having a resort on a paradise island. I wanted that dream, but even in thirty years, I wouldn't realize it as an architect.

I knew I needed a different and quicker path to success. So I decided to quit college to find it.

It was a hard decision, especially because my father had wanted me to be an architect. On the day I made the decision, I phoned my father and said, "Dad, if I'm going to design buildings, it won't be as an architect. It will be as the person who owns the property and has the money to hire the best architects." And I waited for his response.

My dad was surprised and sounded disappointed, but in the end he said, "If that is what you have to do, go do it." I decided to start my own company with a friend, and we began a publishing business with almost no money and even less experience.

That's how I ended up in my late twenties, five years later, living in Singapore and running my little start-up real estate property magazine. So much for making my life an instant success! I had dreams of wild financial success, but that dream's fulfillment still seemed to lie in a hazy, distant future.

This is when I reached a critical moment: I was falling ever deeper into debt. I was working very hard but paying myself very little. I felt like I had no choice: When the company grew, I had to hire another person or pay for extra marketing to grow more. The way I saw it, once the business was successful, it would pay me more. I believed I had to put all the money I made back in the business. The consequences of this decision were about to become clear in a very public way.

As I walked home one evening, lost in thought on the things I had to do tomorrow, I noticed a commotion on our street. Someone was shouting. Actually, it sounded like crying. The neighbors were out watching the drama. As I walked closer, I saw they were looking at the front of *our house*. The one crying was Renate, my wife. Our daughter Kathleen, just a year old and looking very distressed, was in Renate's arms. She was pleading with a man standing in front of a truck—a tow truck lifting our car up by its hook.

I ran toward them. "You can't take our car. Please...," I heard Renate beg. She looked around and saw me.

"What's happening?" I asked.

As if I didn't know: I had been late on the car payments again. Renate had reminded me, and I had promised I would make a payment. But I hadn't. There simply wasn't enough money in the bank. Even though I was keeping up appearances of being successful, in reality I was going into more debt each month, hoping it would all turn around one day. Now our money problems were out there for everyone to see as the man prepared to tow our car away.

"We can pay you tomorrow!" I told the driver.

He just shook his head and handed us a pink slip. "Sign here," he said. "Call the number on the receipt."

I watched him drive off and Renate walk back into the house humiliated. One by one, the neighbors cast me glances of pity and then went back into their homes, too. I was alone now. No money, no car, and no self-respect. Clearly, I had been in denial about my business—ignorant of just how much stress it was causing my wife, my young family, and me.

Standing on that empty street, I made a decision to change my priorities once and for all. *But how?*

It wasn't that I hadn't *tried to change* before. I had read books that talked about paying yourself first, but none of them explained to me how I could make the money to pay myself in a way that was easy and natural for me. I had read books on success, leadership, and wealth creation, but the more I read, the more confused I became: Each new book's advice seemed to contradict the advice in the book I had just finished.

One book stressed the importance of climbing the corporate ladder, while the next said you can't get wealthy from a job and I was better off with my own business. Some told me to follow my passion, while others told me to follow my purpose. Some urged me to be daring and take big, bold risks; some advised me to be cautious and take small steps. Some said the key to wealth was trading shares and options, while others dismissed that entirely and recommended network marketing, online marketing, or property investment.

Head spinning, I looked to business role models instead. That didn't work out any better. Richard Branson wrote that it is all about being the entrepreneur adventurer, but then Jack Welch proved you could reach the top working for others. Oprah Winfrey showed the power of shining from the front with the stars, while Mark Zuckerberg was happy to hack in the back in his hoodie. Warren Buffett and Bill Gates may make great bridge partners, but they had entirely different paths to success: Buffett invests in many businesses but never in anything high-tech; Gates focused his life on growing just one high-tech business.

Truth is, I had no idea what was right for me. And, unable to find any clear direction, I ended up following the most common path: trial and error. That's how I ended up getting my car repossessed. That night, in desperation, I made a decision. Instead of being lost with everyone giving me different advice, I was going to find my own path. That decision led me to find not only my path but also an *entire map* of wealth creation.

Fast-forward a couple of decades, and I'm writing this book— describing what I've learned since that night—from my dream resort in Bali. I have been living here for the better part of a decade, running a string of businesses and mentoring social entrepreneurs who are making an impact around the world.

I've made plenty of decisions, good and bad, to get here. But the quantum leap that put me on this path to wealth creation did not come when I had the dream and began my first business. It was on that evening in Singapore three years later when my car was repossessed, when I committed to the dream *and* a clear plan to get there.

For the first time, I set a personal earning plan and made it more important to me than my business plan. I began to focus on what worked for my strengths. Instead of paying myself less than I needed to survive, and hoping my business would one day make millions, I created a vision and plan in which my personal net cash flow after expenses increased every three months. Within a month, I was cash flow positive. Within six months, by keeping to my plan, I had an extra $500 every month, which I put aside. Over the next two years, I kept to my plan, and my personal cash flow for investments grew to over $10,000 each month. Before I was thirty, I had become a multimillionaire with the money and time to support the people and causes I believe in—simply as a result of changing my focus.

In other words, my quantum leap that night in Singapore was also my first step in discovering this Millionaire Master Plan I'm about to share with you: *to choose my destination and then clear the way to get there.* But while knowing where you want to go is an important part of the Millionaire Master Plan, it won't matter *if you don't know who or where you are.*

That's what the Millionaire Master Plan provides: a GPS to achieve your success. A GPS is more than just a map. It shows you where you are and where you are going, gives you the best routes to take, and plots the specific steps to get there. That is my promise to you: to give you that clarity based on *your* natural path.

From my first business as a teenager to the dozen companies I built, sold, crashed, burned, and grew in my twenties to the thousands of people I mentored and worked with in my thirties, it has become increasingly obvious to me that we all go through the same stages of learning and the same breakthroughs to master each stage of success in our wealth. We are all on the same map, just in different places. This map—the Millionaire Master Plan—isn't just a two-dimensional map of the landscape. It is a three-dimensional blueprint of a building the architect in me designed: *the Wealth Lighthouse.*

The Wealth Lighthouse has nine levels, which link to the nine stages of wealth: Victim, Survivor, Worker, Player, Performer, Conductor, Trustee, Composer, and Legend. Like climbing a mountain, the strategy and equipment you need change the higher you go. You and I are each at one of these levels. What we should do next depends on which level we are at.

But before you can determine what stage or level of the Wealth Lighthouse you are currently on, you must know *which of its four sides to enter*. Each of these sides corresponds to one of the four types of geniuses that create wealth: Dynamo, Blaze, Tempo, and Steel. These geniuses and their connection to the Wealth Lighthouse are what I cover in part 1. Only then can you focus on the second and third parts of this book, which cover the first six levels to develop positive cash flow, design the life you deserve to live, and make the impact you are ready to make.

You see, every one of us has a genius inside us. Once we realize it, we find our own internal guidance system. It turns out the information those books and role models provided when I consulted them years ago were not *wrong*. Neither are any of the wonderful authors writing today. They are all on the same map. Each is the right advice when you are at the right level but will be the wrong advice if you are at a different level or genius.

Direction is different from information. Information is *the entire map*. Direction is *how you get from A to B*. In today's information economy, you don't need more information. You need direction. Using a GPS, getting direction is always possible when you know where you are and where you're going. Right now you need direction that is right for *you*. Not for everyone. Not for me and my genius, *for you and your genius*.

That's why your first *step is to take the Millionaire Master Plan Test right now!*

For the last ten years I have been deciphering this Millionaire

Master Plan while mentoring and working with people from more than eighty countries around the world. In fact, leaders from around the globe have used the guides linked with the Millionaire Master Plan to go from being in debt to generating millions, growing charities that impact millions, increasing their success in their careers, growing the quality time they have with their family, and much more.

That's why I say with confidence that regardless of what you want to do—whether your goal is simply to cut out the stress of money, build wealth to provide for your family, or make your work more meaningful and fulfilling—you will find the steps to take on your personal path on my Millionaire Master Plan.

That's why, before you go farther in the book, you need to use the following instructions to take the Millionaire Master Plan Test and learn your natural genius and lighthouse level.

My final words before we get started are: No one can go through or move up the Wealth Lighthouse alone. In fact, the spark often comes from someone else—someone who complements your genius. You are going to attract that team as you make your journey through the Millionaire Master Plan, and I hope you will share your journey with us, too.

We have a very active global community and provide plenty of support at every level of the Master Plan on our online learning community, GeniusU. You can post your experiences, questions, and comments by going to our Millionaire Master Plan website: www.millionairemasterplan.com.

We are all on a journey together to improve our own wealth and the wealth of those around us. I call this mission World Wide Wealth—our ability to collectively create more and contribute more. In fact, just buying this book means you have already made a difference.

A portion of the proceeds from this book is going toward

providing education and financial literacy to children (and adults) so they can learn the skills they need to advance in this fast-changing world.

Thank you for joining this journey and making an impact in a small but very important way.

Okay, are you ready? Let's make magic.

—Roger

ACTION POINT

Take the Millionaire Master Plan Test!

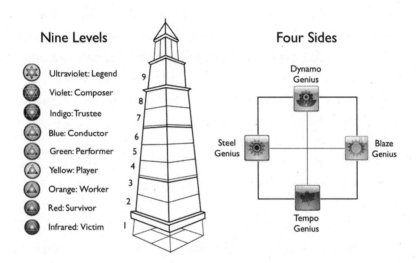

Nine Levels

Ultraviolet: Legend
Violet: Composer
Indigo: Trustee
Blue: Conductor
Green: Performer
Yellow: Player
Orange: Worker
Red: Survivor
Infrared: Victim

Four Sides

Dynamo Genius

Steel Genius

Blaze Genius

Tempo Genius

O n the inside of the back cover flap, there is a code that you can use to take the Millionaire Master Plan Test.

This test is essential for understanding how this book works and following your path through it.

Simply enter the code at www.millionairemasterplan.com to take the test. It only takes about fifteen minutes. After finishing the test, you will receive two reports via email:

- The first report will come immediately and identify which of the four geniuses is your natural genius. This is your compass through this book and the Wealth Lighthouse. The significance of knowing your genius is explained in chapter 1.

- The second report will arrive shortly after and will tell you what level you are currently at in the Wealth Lighthouse. The lighthouse and all its levels are explained in chapter 2.

Why two reports? The Millionaire Master Plan Test is unique in that it measures both personality (your genius) and progress (your wealth level). While your genius will stay the same, your wealth level can move up. Thus I have deliberately divided the test into two parts so that you can come back and take the wealth level part again in the future and track your progress in the coming months and years.

A note for the impatient: If you are the kind of person who is tempted to begin the next part without taking the test, don't! There are two important reasons why.

First, you need to know where you are to know where you're going: How you master each level of the lighthouse and build wealth naturally depends on your genius. What path you take through the steps at each level depends on which genius you are. Chances are you have taken wealth-building advice in the past that has been wrong not only for your level but also for your genius. The advice didn't work, and you ended up wasting precious time and energy. Don't make the same mistake before you begin this book!

Second, you need to be connected: Most challenges in life come from *not* being connected to people we need when we need them. When you go online to take the Millionaire Master Plan Test, you will connect with a community of like-minded people who are already part of GeniusU as well as enjoying access to a variety of free learning resources.

So don't just jump to the next chapter: Use the code on the inside of the back cover flap and go take the test at www.millionaire masterplan.com*!*

PART I

YOUR NATURAL PATH

Your Genius and the Wealth Lighthouse

Everyone is a genius.
But if you judge a fish on its ability to climb a tree,
it will live its whole life believing it is stupid.

YOUR GENIUS

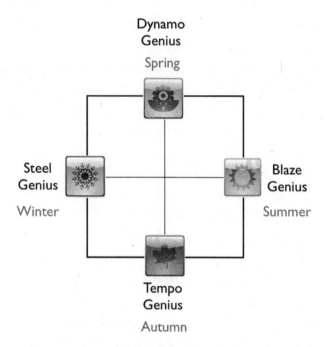

Try this little experiment: Fold your arms. Look whether you have folded your left arm over your right arm or your right over your left.

Now do the opposite: Fold your right arm over your left arm or your left over your right. Does it feel comfortable? For most people, it doesn't; for some, it is even hard to do—it feels... *unnatural*. That's because you're doing the wrong thing. That's not to say there is one right way to fold our arms. There is only your natural way.

We are all born great at something, but as we grow up, we find out all the things that we aren't so good at. So we spend our lives feeling bad about those things, working on our natural weaknesses while we take our natural strengths for granted. This truth is no more tragic than in a school of children, where every child has a different genius, but when they are all judged by the same test, many lose their confidence and with it their desire to learn. *Why try to be something else when you are already naturally you—you are enough!*

When we become aware of our natural genius, it's like a light going on. Suddenly we realize we do not need to focus on our weaknesses to be successful. We simply need to follow a path that plays to our natural strengths. These are the four geniuses:

Dynamo Genius who loves to **Create**
Blaze Genius who loves to **Connect**
Tempo Genius who loves to **Serve**
Steel Genius who loves the **Details**

When you've used the code on the inside of the back cover flap, taken the Millionaire Master Plan Test on www.millionaire masterplan.com, and read your Genius Report, you will know which one of the four you are. But before you proceed, you need to understand how your genius wins by following certain "rules."

The Rules of the Genius Game

By rules, I mean that each genius is like a sport you can become great at. If you know the game you are best suited for and the rules of that game, you can now focus on being the best at it. And here's a truth about sports: Sometimes the rules of one sport are the exact opposite of another sport's. For example, if you're playing soccer, the rule is that you kick the ball; you don't pick it up. In basketball, the rule is that you pick the ball up; you don't kick it.

Similarly, if you're a Blaze Genius and you hold a job that doesn't feature much variety—one in which you sit at your desk all day dealing with the details instead of getting out and connecting with people—you are guaranteed to be miserable whether you're working at your own business or for someone else. But if you are a Steel Genius and you are sent out to meet people every day, you're going to be equally miserable. People, books—even you, yourself—may tell you to keep doing it because "that's your job," but all you do is feel stupid and want to escape the whole thing.

I have seen people struggle to get out of debt because they've been told they need to keep track of every bill, and that isn't their genius's strength. They are trying to follow rules for a game that isn't their natural game! When they discover the rules of their genius, they follow a different strategy that gets them out of debt easily.

I have seen employees yearning to quit their jobs because they are struggling in an environment that is making them miserable, but they don't know how to replace their income with something they love. When they discover their genius, some suddenly see a path forward and have the courage to act, while others simply shift what they are doing in their job and suddenly love their life with a career on the fast track.

What's your genius? I'm a Dynamo Genius, a natural creator. I struggled when it came to managing my own detailed accounts; that's how I ended up cash negative and carless. Only by understanding my genius could I see a path forward that was natural to me, as you will hear in chapter 3.

This is why I say your genius is your compass to navigate the Millionaire Master Plan.

Understanding the Four Geniuses

The idea of these four geniuses dates back five thousand years and connects to the four frequencies found in ancient Chinese and Indian thought. Aristotle and Plato identified them, too. But while the ideas behind these geniuses may be ancient in origin, they are being applied here in a completely new way: to the entrepreneurial spirit and your personal path of least resistance to wealth and success.

As you will see in the tables that follow, each genius has a different way to reach fulfillment. Each has a different way to manage time and money, grow a network, and lead a team. Each genius has a winning and a losing formula, and your winning formula is someone else's losing formula. Each genius also features a frequency you are strongest in and is part of a state of change, like the four seasons.

Our genius connects to how we lead and love. It connects to how we communicate, and how we market ourselves and our products or services differently. This is why one-size-fits-all books that insist you need to do it all and add that there is only one way will often contradict each other. They are like ineffective diets that force you to change who you are—as if a thinner you must be someone else, not simply a healthier version of who you already are. *Think of knowing your genius as the first step in customizing a diet for the perfect you.*

Of course, none of us is only one thing: We all have a little of each genius in us. But we all have more of one than the others. Before you enter the Wealth Lighthouse, the first step to setting yourself free is to truly understand where the compass of each of these geniuses points and how they connect to each other.

Dynamo Geniuses: Ideas Smart

"I believe in benevolent dictatorship provided I am the dictator."

—Richard Branson

Great at...	Creation: Dynamos start and move things forward. They see the future more than anyone else. They succeed with their "heads in the clouds" and short attention spans.
Not so great at...	Finishing, timing, peripheral issues, paying attention: Teachers probably yelled at Dynamos in class for not paying attention.
Winning Formula	Creating value through innovation: Dynamos have creativity, flair, and the ability to get things started. They grow.
Losing Formula	Consultation and relying on intuition. Dynamo Genius is weakest at timing, service, and sensing others—in other words, acting like a Steel Genius.
Opposite Genius	Tempo Genius

Dynamo Geniuses include Richard Branson, Bill Gates, Steve Jobs, Michael Jackson, Beethoven, Thomas Edison, and Albert Einstein. All of these people focused on their strengths in creating. They ignored those who criticized them for not being organized or social enough. They didn't worry about being forgetful or missing the small things. They are all remembered today for their creative brilliance, because they were best at answering the question, *What?*

Blaze Geniuses: People Smart

"In leadership you have to exaggerate every statement you make. You've got to repeat it a thousand times and exaggerate it."

—Jack Welch

Great at...	Conversation and communication: Blazes are all about relationships, putting people first, and talking to those people and hearing their stories. They learn through talking and telling/hearing stories.
Not so great at...	Details: Blazes are weakest at analysis and detailed calculation.
Winning Formula	Creating leverage through magnification: Blazes ask the question, *How can this only be done with me?* They build their brand by growing their relationships. They magnify.
Losing Formula	Calculation: Blazes get stuck when they try and multiply, growing through systems that work without them.
Opposite Genius	Steel Genius

Blaze Geniuses include Bill Clinton, Jack Welch, Oprah Winfrey, Ellen DeGeneres, and Larry King. All of these charismatic people focused on their strengths in leadership and connections. They ignored those who criticized them for not focusing on the numbers or not planning enough. They never worried that they changed focus too often or didn't like being stuck in an office. They just got out there to make a difference through people, with fun and variety, because they were best at answering the question, *Who?*

Tempo Geniuses: Senses Smart

"The ear of the leader must ring with the voices of the people."

—Woodrow Wilson

Great at...	Staying grounded, dealing with lots of activity, being very hands-on, and requiring testimonials and referrals: Don't expect a creative plan from Tempo Geniuses. Do expect them to do what needs to be done on time.
Not so great at...	Innovation, public speaking, strategic planning, and seeing the bigger picture.
Winning Formula	Creating value through timing: Tempos don't need to create anything if they know when to buy, when to sell, when to act, and when to hold.
Losing Formula	Creativity: Tempos are weakest when they try and innovate from a blank sheet, trying to create their way to success instead of using their natural senses.
Opposite Genius	Dynamo Genius

Tempo Geniuses include Warren Buffett, George Soros, Woodrow Wilson, Gandhi, Nelson Mandela, Mother Teresa, and Michael Phelps. All of these people focused on their strengths in their senses and perseverance. They ignored those who criticized them for not being more forceful or politically astute. They didn't worry that they liked being extra careful and wanted to take more time over things. They just stayed calm and grounded, taking their time, because they were best at answering the question, *When?*

Steel Geniuses: Details Smart

"The quality of a leader is reflected in the standards they set for themselves."

—Ray Kroc

Great at...	Calculation: Steels love handbooks, manuals, and reading through small print to understand and clarify all the information. Steels will take their time and get things right. They won't be rushed and will carefully create systems to build their flow.
Not so great at...	Small talk and constant communication.
Winning Formula	Creating leverage through multiplication: Steels ask the question, *How can this be done without me?* Through systems they make things simple and make many and multiply.
Losing Formula	Communication: Steels often suck the energy out of a Dynamo (their metal axes chop down a Dynamo's wood), and too much contact with a Blaze can dull their sharp minds (fire can melt a metal).
Opposite Genius	Blaze Genius

Steel Geniuses include famous entrepreneurs such as John D. Rockefeller, Henry Ford, Ray Kroc, Larry Page, Sergey Brin, and Mark Zuckerberg. All of these people focused on their strengths in systems and in managing data. They ignored those who criticized them for not having better social skills or being more sensitive. They didn't worry that they often liked being alone and often did their best work when locked away. They just kept focused on finding smarter ways to do things through their systems, because they were best at answering the question, *How?*

The Key to Wealth Is Flow

Understanding your genius helps you find the right books and role models. It gives you clarity on what to say yes and no to. Most important, in part 2 you will see your genius is your path of least resistance to rise through the Wealth Lighthouse. It allows you to find your flow—not in a month, or a year. Right now. Today.

All living systems flow. Our bodies naturally flow. Talent flows, products flow, information flows. So does wealth, and when flow crosses flow, wealth grows. Just think of this in terms of commerce: Ships were launched, lines of flow converged at ports on coasts and rivers, and capital cities grew. When roads and rails connected those ports, flows crossed and wealth grew. Today the world's wealthiest people can be found where the greatest flow intersects.

So what does flow have to do with your genius and success? Everything! *When you know your genius, you can get in your flow and then make that flow grow stronger.*

Think about the times in your life when everything has felt like hard work: These were the moments when you were focusing on your weaknesses and your losing formula. Think about the times in your life when everything flowed with effortless ease: Here you were following your natural genius and your winning formula. Now think about teaming up with geniuses with strengths and winning formulas that balance your weaknesses and losing formula; *that's* the key to getting in flow.

In this way, your genius is not only a compass but also the flame of a candle. Too often we focus our energy on the wax of that candle, not the flame. When we focus on trying to get more wax, it is a zero-sum game. For me to have more wax means you have less wax. For one person to get richer means the other person gets poorer. When we focus on the flame, however, our results become exponential. It costs a candle nothing to light another candle. As we light those around us, we realize we have lost nothing but our shadows. We realize that's the point of a candle.

That's both the purpose we find and the fulfillment we feel as we rise up the Wealth Lighthouse.

When you know the genius of your friends, your colleagues, your boss, and your family, you can appreciate *them* for what they are best at and bring out the best in them. As for the things you're not so great at? There are geniuses to support you who have strengths where you are weakest. Flow is not just about what you hold on to; it is also about what you let go of.

A year and a half after my car was repossessed, I had another quantum leap when I first grasped this key concept. This one was *a million-dollar quantum leap.* I had become cash positive, but as a Dynamo Genius I was struggling to manage the day-to-day operations of my business. I didn't want to have to keep on meeting people and selling ad space every day; I wanted to be innovating and using my creativity more. That's when my friend Patrick dropped by and casually said, "I'm going to go get a million dollars."

Patrick was a real estate agent and had had successful businesses in the past. He said the million dollars would be for a new start-up he planned to launch. At the time, my business was scraping along making about $30,000 in sales each month. I was taking a salary that just covered our rent and basic expenses. But at least my stressed business was a *real* business compared with Patrick's start-up idea. How could he possibly raise a million dollars? I simply did not believe him.

When Patrick urged me to do the same, I ignored him. I was too busy working to take him seriously. In fact, the speed at which I dismissed him was almost as blinding as the speed at which I fell off my chair less than six weeks later when he came back with that million-dollar check.

It turned out Patrick had read in the newspaper that a local angel investor was investing in promising new high-tech businesses by writing checks for a million dollars. Patrick's plan had been to meet this investor, find out what kind of business would be his perfect business to invest in, and then put together a plan to launch his start-up as exactly that kind of business. His strategy had been the right one: Find the investors you want to work with and understand the criteria they use to make their investments.

I remember on the day Patrick got his check, I went home and thought I had been doing it all wrong. There were trillions of dollars flowing around the world each day, like water flowing through rivers. I had been digging in a desert—how would I ever tap into flow doing that? I would never raise the money to grow my business and pay myself by relying on my creativity alone. If I could use my natural Dynamo Genius strengths to do what my friend Patrick (who was also a Dynamo Genius) had done to secure his venture capital, surely I could tap into this flow of wealth as well?

I made a commitment to give it a go. My first challenge was my time. I had been managing my business myself because I had been using the excuse that I couldn't afford anyone to help me. With this new commitment, I asked myself an essential question: *Can I afford someone better than me by paying him later?* I looked for a publishing professional who could help me manage my business. That's when I found Peter Watkins, a Blaze Genius and a publishing veteran ten years my senior working in a large publishing group.

I told Peter about my plan to raise capital for my business. I asked him if he would be willing to take a leap of faith and become general manager of my business at a fraction of his current pay. I used my Dynamo Genius to show him a plan where I could raise the money to take us to the next level of growth while he used his Blaze Genius to manage the business and improve what I had started. Together, we could share in a company with more resources and better prospects than each of us had today. His Blaze energy made the most of my Dynamo energy and allowed us both to achieve more than we could on our own.

Peter joined the company and freed up my time. Within a month, with plan in hand, I was knocking on the doors of venture capital firms. Within three months, I got a $3 million commitment from the firm 3i. It was the biggest check I had ever seen. I remember photocopying it (enlarging it to as big a size as the photocopier would allow) and then pinning it on the wall. I remember thinking how hard I had been working just three months earlier, when I had been working against my natural genius, trying to push water uphill instead of going with the flow.

It was of course not as easy as I am making it sound. That level of detail is for the next part of the book. Even so, it surprised me how quickly I went from my day-to-day activity of meeting clients and selling magazines with thousands of dollars in flow to meeting investors and selling part of my business with millions of dollars in flow. It was not how hard I was working that changed. (Geniuses work hard; it just doesn't feel like work when they are in their flow.) It was the level of flow around me that changed.

This is even true in our personal relationships. My wife, Renate, is a Tempo Genius. We are opposites! We have been married for more than twenty years, but in our first years together we didn't realize our genius lay in those differences. I would always wonder why she wasn't willing to take greater risks. She was always wondering why I kept starting new things. These differences would often lead to arguments as we judged each other by our own natural tendencies.

When we became aware of our opposing geniuses, we came to appreciate and understand each other. We realized we were trying to take each other out of our own flow. Renate now lets me have my crazy inventor moments, and I know she needs time to process new information, so I won't put her on the spot or ask for an immediate decision on things. We both support each other to stay in flow.

The Fifth Frequency

There is a fifth frequency that links the four geniuses into a learning cycle. This fifth frequency is what Aristotle called "the first mover" or the source to the rest. This is water energy, which is the basis of flow. The five frequencies form a cycle that begins and ends at water. Every project, business, industry, and country goes through these frequencies as they cycle from creation to completion to creation again.

You are currently going through this natural cycle with each relationship you have and each journey you embark on. It is your entrepreneurial spirit. It is the beginning of every cycle. It is the question *Why?* that leads to the questions asked by each of the other frequencies: *What?* (Dynamo), *Who?* (Blaze), *When?* (Tempo), and *How?* (Steel).

We will see this learning cycle appear together with the geniuses and at every one of the steps within the Wealth Lighthouse.

CHAPTER ONE SUMMARY

You are a genius: This natural genius is your compass to navigate the Millionaire Master Plan. When you follow your genius compass, you find your flow.

Dynamo Geniuses are ideas smart

Blaze Geniuses are people smart

Tempo Geniuses are senses smart

Steel Geniuses are details smart

Flow is the key to wealth: The more we follow our genius and grow our flow, the more wealth we create.

There is a fifth frequency that links the four geniuses and asks the question, *Why?* that leads to the questions asked by each of the other frequencies: *What?* (Dynamo), *Who?* (Blaze), *When?* (Tempo), and *How?* (Steel).

ACTION POINT

*Create Your Future Vision and
Flight Path!
Think it. Ink it. Do it. Review it.*

To get direction, you need to be clear on not only where you are but also where you are going. That's why you need to create a clear Future Vision. So why is it so few people have one?

"I have too many problems today to think about where I'll be going tomorrow."

"I don't want to disappoint myself by dreaming of something that won't happen."

"I need more clarity before deciding on which way to go."

In my mentoring, I often hear excuses like these. But the failure to set a clear destination is the trigger to every stress and uncertainty we face. The compass of your genius and the map of the Wealth Lighthouse won't help if you don't know where *you* want to go.

Your Future Vision defines your destination and paints a picture of your perfect life in the coming year—imagine it as creating your masterpiece! Once you have set your Future Vision, you set your Flight Path through it with quarterly milestones. Between them and your Millionaire Master Plan Test results, you will have a clear picture of where you are and where you are going during the next year.

Create Your Future Vision

Your Future Vision is about more than just setting goals, more than just visualization. It is about creating a holistic blueprint of what you believe your life will grow into in one year—an immediate future in your control.

Plan a Future Vision that stretches you and excites you—but not so much that you don't believe it's possible. According to Napoleon Hill, this was a big part of the "secret" of America's first billionaires and greatest entrepreneurs he interviewed in *Think and Grow Rich*. Andrew Carnegie, Thomas Edison, Alexander Graham Bell, Henry Ford, John D. Rockefeller... Hill discovered that all of them had one thing in common: an unwavering belief in the future reality they were creating. It wasn't a matter of whether it would happen; it was a matter of when.

I started my first Future Vision the night my car was repossessed. I have written one every year since. I write it in my journal, and I make it very specific, using the powers of hindsight and gratitude. Here's how:

Hindsight: Imagine yourself one year in the future and write a journal entry as your future self, looking back at the last year, beginning, *"In the last year I have..."* Imagining yourself already at your destination, looking back, is far easier than trying to look forward.

Gratitude: In looking back, I do *not* write the line, *"I feel so successful and accomplished because I have achieved..."* Instead, I write with an energy powered by gratitude: "*I am so grateful for the last year. In the last year I have....*"

With hindsight and gratitude, you will feel fulfilled and energized simply by writing your Future Vision. Don't skip ahead, do it *now*! Throw yourself fully into this exercise. Give yourself a good thirty minutes to one hour.

Begin with the date a year from today and write your journal entry. Use the prompts I've given below and include all aspects of your life. How do you want each area of your life to look one year from today? (Add extra paragraphs to include other important areas of your life that you think about.) Be as specific as you can, and share the story of how you got from where you are today to where you will be.

Your entire journal entry could be two pages or ten. When you have completed it, ask yourself if it inspires you. If not, ask what you need to add. Once complete, post a copy where it will be visible to you throughout the coming year. This is your destination for the next twelve months!

Date: ....

> I am so grateful for the last year.
> In the last year I have ...
> My personal cash flow has ...
> My assets have ...
> My time has ...
> My job/business has ...
> My team has ...
> My customers have ...
> My partners have ...
> My health has ...
> My family has ...
> My friends have ...

My sense of purpose has...
My contribution has...
My upcoming year will...

Set Your Flight Path

The second step after creating your one-year Future Vision is to break it up into quarterly milestones. This helps you pace yourself and keep on track. I have quarterly milestones for my life and for each of my businesses.

There is a simple format you can use to divide your Future Vision into quarterly milestones: What did you set as the monthly income you wanted in a year's time? Divide the increase into four. What does that mean you already want your monthly income to be three months from now? Six months from now?

Look at what you have said you will be doing with your time in twelve months. If you were already a quarter of the way there in three months, what would be different? What would it look like six months from now? Don't worry yet about how you will achieve these goals, just focus on *what* and *when*.

I have provided you with a free Flight Path Plan and weekly score tracker on your personal page at www.millionairemaster plan.com. Fill it out and set a time every week to check your progress. I recommend setting aside Sunday evening after dinner to sit for an hour, review your progress, and preview the week ahead against your overall Flight Path. That's what I have done for the last twenty-five years, and this rhythm for success is now as natural as eating and sleeping. I call these my Score Sessions, which plays on three definitions of the word *score*:

- Composition (like a musical score—a way to see my masterpiece on paper)

- Measurement (of my progress like a numeric score)
- Groove (like scoring a piece of wood to make a deeper impression each week)

If you are not sure how to design your Score Session, you will see that I have provided you with a personal guide to running your Score Session successfully on your personal page. Set your Score Session now, put it in your diary, and commit to it!

Enjoy the process!

THE WEALTH LIGHTHOUSE

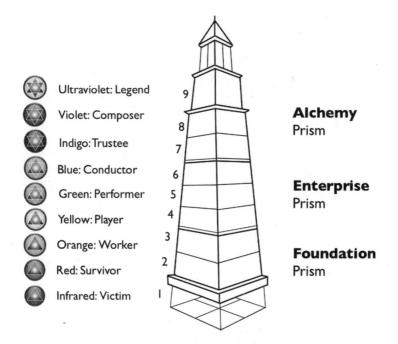

Ultraviolet: Legend

Violet: Composer

Indigo: Trustee

Blue: Conductor

Green: Performer

Yellow: Player

Orange: Worker

Red: Survivor

Infrared: Victim

Alchemy
Prism

Enterprise
Prism

Foundation
Prism

J ust like the origins of the four geniuses, the structures that create the Wealth Lighthouse date back five thousand years to ancient China and India and then draw a path through ancient Egypt, Greece, and Rome up into the time of the Renaissance and the Age of Enlightenment, then through to the modern day. The Wealth Lighthouse has four sides that are connected to the four geniuses we just covered and is made up of nine color-coded ascending levels of wealth (evenly divided into three wealth prisms) that make up the Wealth Spectrum.

These nine levels follow the familiar order of the colors of the rainbow with invisible levels at the bottom (Infrared before Red) and top (Ultraviolet above Violet):

The Foundation Prism (Mastering Your Personal Flow)

Infrared Level: Victim
Red Level: Survivor
Orange Level: Worker

The Enterprise Prism (Mastering Market Flow)

Yellow Level: Player
Green Level: Performer
Blue Level: Conductor

The Alchemy Prism (Mastering Global Flow)

Indigo Level: Trustee
Violet Level: Composer
Ultraviolet Level: Legend

When you took the Millionaire Master Plan Test, you received the second part of your report and you know which is your level in the Wealth Lighthouse. When you learn what level you are at, you are going to be tempted to jump straight to the section below and then the chapter of the book that covers your level. That's okay! Jump straight to your level and read it if you like. You will find in that chapter the steps that suit your genius and the other three geniuses.

But after you read your level, come back and read the levels you missed and learn the important steps that connect each of them. This will help you build your team and understand how to help everyone from your family to friends, partners, and clients— all of whom will be at different levels. You will also learn how your level compares with the other nine levels of wealth, and how the winning formulas at each level are often the losing formula to move to the next level.

You might also be tempted to skip *ahead* of your current level. I know I would be. I'd say, "Sure, I get this. It's all good. I just want to get to the point where I make the millions." *Don't.* There is a discipline that comes at the Infrared Level and every level on up the lighthouse, which is like good plumbing. If you're going to go out and make a million dollars, you'd better make sure your plumbing doesn't leak, because as fast as you make it, you'll lose it just as quickly.

In fact, that's exactly what I did when I was in Infrared Level the day my car was repossessed. I was in denial and wanted to skip the whole Infrared part. I did not know it but I was aiming for Enterprise Prism with all my leaky pipes: looking good and going nowhere.

We each have a voice in our head that is our personal guidance system. We're like pilots in a cockpit who can hear a voice coming from the control tower. The Wealth Lighthouse is like that control tower, and the voice we hear will give entirely different advice depending on which level we are at and which side we are looking out of. As we change levels, the voice from the tower changes in clarity: As we rise higher, the view gets clearer; as we fall, it gets more fuzzy. That's why even the best leaders can get stuck at a level for years, until they make their quantum leap by taking steps necessary to move up a level.

Got it? Okay, let's look inside the lighthouse for a summary of its nine levels and three prisms and what lies ahead. Read them in the context of where you currently are, and where you plan to be.

The Foundation Prism

The foundation of the Wealth Lighthouse is about mastery of our wealth: our ability to create an abundant flow of value and money through our lives regardless of market conditions. These three levels lead us from being in debt to surviving to becoming cash flow positive. The majority of people in the world are working hard at one of these three levels without knowing how to move higher and *stay* higher. Too often, people try to start a business or make investments and end up in a worse position than they started in. By understanding how to build solid foundations at these levels, we stop ourselves from constantly slipping back to the same level in life.

The following three levels make up the Foundation Prism.

Infrared Level: Victim—"Every month, I go deeper and deeper in debt"

Like me the day my car was repossessed in Singapore, Infrared Geniuses fall deeper in debt month after month. Infrared is a horrible feeling of stress, anxiety, and confusion. It is the land of lost geniuses, where you struggle to connect your genius with the world. It's like putting on Infrared goggles—all you can see are the heat waves. You may find yourself in Infrared because you are out of a job, you have gotten into too much debt, or you have overinvested in your properties or business. Some people sell their business and have millions of dollars in assets, but still fall into Infrared because their monthly income becomes negative.

The good news is that anyone and everyone can get out of Infrared within three months by taking specific, drastic action. The Infrared strategy involves turning a "leaky plumbing system" (leaking not just money, but time and energy) into a million-dollar plumbing system, where all your efforts result in success and fulfillment. The payoff of moving to Red Level is that you buy back your time, reclaim your life, and put an end to the constant stress and uncertainty. Much of this action, as you will see, is counterintuitive, and the same steps that get you out of Infrared Level will keep you out of Infrared Level for life. So don't skip this level.

Red Level: Survivor—"I have just enough money to survive"

At the Red Level, you make just enough money to have nothing: Your wages only just cover your lifestyle. Maybe it is because like me in my publishing business, you are focused on putting any money you make into growing your business instead of into growing your own personal wealth. Maybe you have bought a property or shares only to find the money you invested isn't making money, so you are still just surviving. No matter how much more you make, it keeps just disappearing. The result? You feel like you're floating in the sea with your head just above water.

The steps that will move you out of Red Level are at the heart of building your own wealth. They are about putting the center of gravity of your wealth creation on yourself. This is all about increasing self-worth and decreasing self-denial. It is about switching from the winning formula out of Infrared (tapping into your discipline) to the winning formula out of Red (tapping into your deepest passion) to obtain positive cash flow and a rhythm that leads to daily fulfillment.

Orange Level: Worker—"I work hard to earn a living"

Orange Level works for a living. If you are at Orange, you may be in a job, or you may even be self-employed. You have extra money at the end of each month, but you are still chasing the money or chasing the business. At this final level in the Foundation Prism, you have a strong work ethic but are wondering how to turn all this effort into a higher level of income.

Your winning formula—applying yourself passionately to doing good work—is simply not enough to move into the Enterprise Prism and Yellow Level. At the next level up, the Yellow Player is the opposite of the Orange Player. Instead of chasing the ball on the soccer field, at the Yellow Level you choose a team and take a position where others pass the ball to you. People find you instead of you needing to find them. That means you shift from action to attraction. You create a unique identity and master your market. You learn to determine your value, test and measure, and build your personal brand.

The Enterprise Prism

When we master the Foundation Prism, we earn the right to move into the Enterprise Prism. Its levels are about mastery of the wealth flowing through our markets: our ability to manage investments and enterprises effectively to flow value and money through our teams and markets. This is the progress from being securely employed or self-employed to knowing how to excel on a high-performing team to managing multiple teams and multiple streams. More than $4 trillion is moving across this planet and changing hands every single day. How do you get more involved in this flow so you can direct more of it to the things you care about and the impact you want to make?

The three levels of the Enterprise Prism are all linked to music: the Player (who is one person doing all things), the Performer (where all people are doing one thing), and the Conductor (who makes music without needing to play any of the instruments).

Yellow Level: Player—"I love what I do and create my own flow"

If you are at the Yellow Level, you forge your journey. You have built a reputation and have business coming your way. You may be employed, working as a contractor, or self-employed. You know how to attract business, and you know how to create, price, and promote a new product or service. The challenge at this level is that everything revolves around you. While you have a level of freedom, your income still relies on you showing up. The money stops when you stop, just like the music stops when the guitar player stops playing.

The steps out of Yellow Level are the opposite of what got you here: You relied on independence to get here and need to switch to interdependence to get out. The identity and rhythm of your enterprise become more important than your own identity and rhythm. This takes more than just creating systems for your job or your life. It takes leadership and a focus on choosing the right talent. Most important, it means giving up on the idea that only you can do what needs to be done.

Green Level: Performer—"I create flow through team and rhythm"

Green enables enterprises. Leading a team profitably is entirely different from self-employment, but the rewards are exponential. The focus is no longer on you, but on others. The question is no longer how you make money, but how you help others make money. You know how to grow your wealth by connecting to the right team or partnership. You are a leader who is connected to your genius. This was my big jump after Patrick inspired me to go out and tap into the flow of wealth around me to grow my team and regain my time.

Your winning formula is in building the culture of your team and connecting team members to your mission. When you move from Green to Blue Level, you build your ability to manage multiple teams. You have the authority and expertise to attract the right leaders to your various teams and revenue streams. You can own multiple businesses and assets that are all managed effectively. Too many people attempt to reach this level too early, aiming for multiple streams of income before they know how to manage those multiple streams.

Blue Level: Conductor—"I have multiple teams and multiple streams"

Blue Level frees you entirely from having your hands full. You have multiple investments, and you have mastered both cash and capital. Like an orchestra conductor, you can now make the music without needing to play any instruments. Also like an orchestra conductor, you are not facing your audience, but facing your performers.

I, like you, am on a journey. Right now, I am at Blue Level, where an understanding of a balance sheet and assets trumps an understanding of profitability and performance. Of course, I could choose to stay at this level for the rest of my life as one of many invisible millionaires. But I am striving to move up to Indigo Level, where I can make a bigger difference in the world by helping to empower others. An Indigo Trustee must earn the right to move millions via the trust of their market. Many of the highest-profile wealth creators in the world have chosen this step. Their trust and track record in their market are so high that people will pay millions just for the right to invest in their businesses or partner with them, because they are reliable and trustworthy spokespeople for those markets or missions.

The Alchemy Prism

This is the prism in which the rules of our markets are created. This is mastery of the wealth flowing through our societies. Many wealth creation books are more focused on "working the system" than on "changing the system." Yet many of the highest-profile wealth creators today, including Warren Buffett, Bill Gates, Richard Branson, and Oprah Winfrey, have earned the right, by stepping up the levels, to actively change the system in their own ways and change things on a global scale.

Few people reach this third prism. It is the least understood but most important prism within the Wealth Spectrum. This is the prism in which our money is printed, our laws are passed, and the rules by which we play the game are made. There was a time when this prism was outside our domain; governments took charge of these levels. More recently, we began to realize we each have the power to make a difference in the world, but we need to earn the right to do so. Do you have friends or colleagues who tell you they have a mission to change the world? The truth is, they can, but first they need to earn the credibility and follow through the steps of the lighthouse.

While I am not yet in the Alchemy Prism, I plan to be. We are both on the same journey through this lighthouse, and I hope we will get to share this journey in the coming years. So the final part of this book will briefly outline the levels of the Alchemy Prism and how we can make the biggest difference in our lifetimes:

Indigo Level: Trustee—"I have the trust of my market"

Indigo Level is the playground of the multimillionaire and billionaire. When you have mastered the Enterprise Prism, trust becomes your greatest asset, and one that you can monetize in magical ways.

Violet Level: Composer—"I make the rules of the game"

Violet Level prints our currencies, sets our taxes, and scripts the tunes we dance to. Until recently this was the domain of nations, but now more entrepreneurs, leaders, and communities are stepping into the role of composer and rewriting the rules.

Ultraviolet Level: Legend—"I am a symbol of my time"

Ultraviolet is the final level. In a rainbow, it is above the visible spectrum. Those people at this level are the symbols to live by, like legends on a map. Their names become synonymous with their composition and are left as a legacy.

Why We Get Stuck at Each Level

Have you ever met someone stuck in a job, dreaming of being their own boss but never making the move? Or have you met someone who made the move only to find the formula that made them a great employee is now making them a terrible entrepreneur? Have you ever met someone who grew a small business to earn their freedom only to find they can't even afford to take a holiday?

Do you have friends who have been in these situations, but later had a breakthrough and found that the invisible ceiling they were bumping against year after year magically disappeared? They can always pinpoint afterward the shift in mind-set and actions they went through. They will always tell you they needed to let go of something and adopt a whole new set of rules, which led to a whole new set of actions.

As we progress along our entrepreneurial and business paths, every one of us reaches a moment when, no matter how hard we try, we cannot move ahead with the same strategy that got us there. Think of the gears in a car: Putting our foot on the accelerator while still in a lower level is no longer the answer to moving faster into the next level. Shifting from one level to the next means letting go of our winning formula and learning an entirely new one. In other words, going faster in this "car" means taking your foot *off* the accelerator in order to change gears. You need to disengage the clutch, let the car freewheel (even if only for a few seconds), and reengage with an entirely new gear—a gear that until that point was not even being used.

There is a good chance that as you look at the people around you who are at different levels than you, and you read even these short descriptions of the levels and how we get stuck, you will nod knowingly and say, "I've been trying to tell them that for so long, but they just won't listen." Why is it that it can seem so obvious to us what others could do to move out of their level, but it still feels so difficult for us to move ourselves?

The reason is, we enjoy a freedom at our current level that unconsciously we do not want to let go of.

In the Foundation Prism, as an **Infrared Victim** I could see that (in theory) with more discipline and application I could move to Red Level. But I didn't want to give up my *freedom of choice* to spend my time and money the way I wanted to.

When I got to **Red Survivor** by giving up my freedom of choice with a more disciplined routine that made me the money I needed to survive, I gained freedom of movement. I was less stressed and more able to make use of my Dynamo Genius. But to move to **Orange Worker** meant being even more accountable to serving others and fitting in to their schedule. That meant losing the one thing I had fought for at Red Level: my *freedom of movement*.

When I got to **Orange Worker**, what I gained was a new level of freedom of choice. Many opportunities came my way that weren't there before. But then to move up to Yellow Level meant focusing on a niche, which meant giving up this *freedom of choice* I had just fought for! I would need to say no to many of the opportunities coming my way.

It gets even harder when we move into the Enterprise Prism. As a **Yellow Player** I gained a freedom of movement to do what I wanted and go where I wanted—the kind of freedom that Tim Ferriss talks about in *The 4-Hour Workweek*. To move to Green Level meant building a team, a schedule, and accountability. I would need to give up the *freedom of movement* I was enjoying.

When I committed to creating the rhythm and model necessary to attract a team, as a **Green Performer** I gained a new freedom of choice that comes from a sustainable businesses that does not depend on any one person—the kind of choice that Jim Collins talks about in *From Good to Great*. Higher-level opportunities came our way. But to move to Blue Level meant giving up that *freedom of choice* to select my team and decide how the business would work. I would need to leave that to others who would run my businesses for me.

In becoming a **Blue Conductor** and having others lead my businesses for me, I could no longer choose what I could change in my businesses; instead I empowered others to make those decisions for me. But with multiple streams of income, I gained an even higher level of freedom of movement. At this level, the higher calling to be an Indigo Trustee for your industry or cause inevitably arrives. At this point, you need to ask if you are willing to give up that *freedom of movement* you have earned to live up to the higher public expectations of being a role model for or leader of your industry or cause.

Notice a pattern? In the nine steps up the Wealth Lighthouse, we move in a zigzag from freedom of choice to freedom of movement. We progress through personal value and personal leverage to social value and social leverage. At each step we move from the driver (who knows how to drive the vehicle but not how to build it) to the designer (who knows how to design the vehicle).

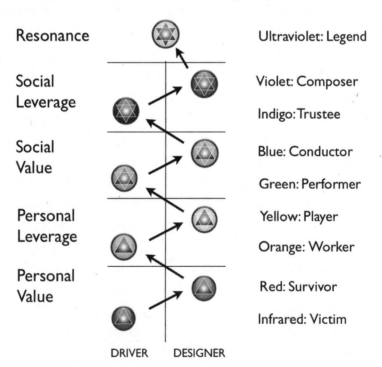

Resonance		Ultraviolet: Legend
Social Leverage		Violet: Composer
		Indigo: Trustee
Social Value		Blue: Conductor
		Green: Performer
Personal Leverage		Yellow: Player
		Orange: Worker
Personal Value		Red: Survivor
		Infrared: Victim
DRIVER	DESIGNER	

In giving up freedom of movement or freedom of choice, we are sacrificing the reason we fought so hard to get to that level. The books on financial freedom seduced us when we were at Red Level. We were seduced by the books on freedom to travel the world when we moved to Yellow Level. We loved the idea of building a lasting legacy when we moved to Green Level.

But remember this: At every level, we may have to give up on choice or movement, but we never give up freedom itself—the freedom we have earned in order to earn the right to move to the next level and how great it feels to do it in our natural genius state. It feels, well, freeing!

Also remember you are never alone. While each of the four geniuses takes a different path through these levels, there are four fundamental truths for all of us regardless of our genius or what level we are on:

1. **We are all in the Wealth Spectrum:** All economic conditions—from being in debt to being a millionaire to controlling a country's taxes to being a global philanthropist—exist in the nine levels of the Wealth Spectrum. We are all at one of the nine levels.

2. **All the levels are connected:** We change levels through our life. Each level jumps up naturally to the next, like gears in a car. Understanding the nine levels and where you are empowers you to ensure your path to your success is deliberate and not accidental.

3. **Your level determines your reality:** Every level has a level of flow and a level of consciousness. When we move levels, our flow changes and so does our awareness. The problems and opportunities you see in life will depend on both your genius and how that genius flows in the level you are at. When you change level, you change what you see and who you attract but not who you are.

4. **You choose your level:** Your wealth is your choice. When you know your level, you can choose to stay at that level, move down, or move up. Each has costs and benefits. Knowing your level gives you the power to direct your focus on the next steps to take. You are always only at one level at any one time, and seeing all levels will give you a full picture of where you want to (and don't want to) be playing.

So let's get to it. You have the basic sense of this map and the GPS. You have your Millionaire Master Plan assessments and know who you are (your genius) and where you are (your level) as you move through the Wealth Lighthouse. You have created your Future Vision and Flight Path. Now the steps through the lighthouse levels begin.

CHAPTER TWO SUMMARY

Whether deep in debt or on the verge of becoming a millionaire and changing the world, **we are all part of the Wealth Lighthouse**.

There are nine levels of wealth in the Wealth Lighthouse, divided into three Wealth Prisms. We are often stuck on a level because we are working at an old strategy from a lower level, or we are trying to work at a strategy from a higher level we are not yet ready for:

The Foundation Prism is our mastery of flow in our life.

Level One—Infrared Victim: You fall deeper in debt month after month.

Level Two—Red Survivor: You make just enough money to have nothing.

Level Three—Orange Worker: You have to work hard to earn a living.

The Enterprise Prism is the mastery of flow in our markets.

Level Four—Yellow Player: Your earnings are limited, because you and your enterprises still rely on you more than others.

Level Five—Green Performer: You enable enterprises. Your rewards are exponential, leading to high-performance teams and enterprises.

Level Six—Blue Conductor: You have multiple investments and have mastered both cash and capital. You think in millions.

The Alchemy Prism is the master of flow in our societies.

Level Seven—Indigo Trustee: This is the playground of the billionaire where trust becomes your greatest asset and one that you can monetize in magical ways.

Level Eight—Violet Composer: At this level you print our currencies, set our taxes, and script the tunes we dance to.

Level Nine—Ultraviolet Legend: People here are symbols to live by, like legends on a map.

Next Steps

Watch the online videos: When you visit the website www.millionairemasterplan.com, you will find there are videos at each level of the Wealth Spectrum. Watch the videos that are most relevant to you. Understanding the levels will prepare you for the content in the chapters ahead.

Complete the Preflight Checklist that follows this chapter.

ACTION POINT

Checklist Check-In

It's essential that you review the Preflight Checklists found at the end of each chapter from here on before you begin work on the following chapter. I call them Preflight Checklists because they are like the checklists pilots go through before they take off—lists that even the most experienced pilot will complete every flight without fail.

Use these checklists to remind yourself of the steps at each level through the Millionaire Master Plan, and use them regularly enough that the review becomes habit. Every week, I go through all my Preflight Checklists in order from the beginning through my current level. It only takes about ten minutes and becomes part of my weekly meditation for the week ahead.

Don't do this and you'll learn what I did early on: Most loss of wealth comes from carelessness, when you stray from your "flight path" (or forget to set one) and stop looking at your instruments. You can't predict all the external conditions and internal challenges on your flights, but you can correct yourself and stay on course.

These checklists parallel the Playbooks linked to your personal page on the Millionaire Master Plan website that move you through every level of the Wealth Lighthouse. This book and its Preflight Checklists serve as gateways to these Playbooks. Starting with chapter 3, I will include one action step after each chapter of the book; follow this and you can check at least one Preflight Checklist box yes.

Below is your first Preflight Checklist. If you did the Action Point following chapter 1 and completed your Future Vision and Flight Path, you can already check two of the following checklist boxes yes.

Preflight Checklist: Infrared Level

1. I have a written, inspiring Future Vision of where I will be that is visible and front-of-mind.   ☐ Yes   ☐ No

2. I have a Flight Path that gives me monthly personal and financial milestones to achieve my Future Vision.   ☐ Yes   ☐ No

3. I follow a rhythm to review my Future Vision and Flight Path to ensure that I self-correct and stay on track.   ☐ Yes   ☐ No

PART II

THE FOUNDATION PRISM

Level 1—Infrared Level: Victim
Level 2—Red Level: Survivor
Level 3—Orange Level: Worker

Scaling these levels leads to a mastery of the wealth flowing through our lives. It lets us create abundant flows of value and money regardless of market conditions.

Wealth isn't how much money you have.
Wealth is what you're left with if you lose all your money.

FROM INFRARED TO RED: VICTIM TO SURVIVOR

Measure:	Negative personal cash flow every month
Emotions:	Struggle; blame; denial
Cost of staying here:	Stress; anxiety; helplessness
Focus needed:	Discipline and duty
How did I get here?	Not paying attention; not knowing better; not controlling flow
How do I move up?	Measure Your Money; Commit to Conduct; Do Your Duty

Have you ever gotten into a shower that's the perfect temperature and then *Boom!* it's boiling hot and then *Boom!* it's freezing cold? You jump out of the shower but no matter how much you try, you can't get it right. Infrared is that experience with money, with your personal cash flow going backward every month. To get out of it, we need to get some good plumbing in place that gives us a level of predictability so that we can actually learn how to make the extra money we need on a weekly basis to survive and move to Red Level.

People at Infrared either don't know how to do that or think they do know and want it to be much bigger *right now*. They say, "Why would I want to make an extra $100 a week when I can be out there trying to get $10,000 or more?"

That was my experience early on with my publishing business. I was at this level when my car was repossessed. My business was generating some revenue, but I wasn't paying myself enough to survive. "I'm not going to worry about that," I said. "I'm not going to pay myself now; I'm just going to go for bigger stuff. I don't need to worry about making a couple of thousand dollars to pay for my car, because I'm going to be a millionaire. Why would I need that?"

Simply put, I was in denial—a core part of the disconnected state of Infrared. Infrared is below the visible color spectrum: You can't see its heat waves, which eat you away from the inside. But with your Infrared goggles on, all you can see are those heat waves; you can't see anything else clearly. Thus, it is extremely difficult to make good decisions because you do not have any reference points to work from.

And the consequences—as I learned that night in Singapore as I saw my car getting towed away—are more than just negative cash flow.

Why Infrared Kills

It's the stress, panic, and uncertainty each day brings that make Infrared such a state of emergency. People around us can sense when we're Infrared. Our actions, thoughts, and language are different. Like all people at Infrared Level, every time I fell into it, I was exhausted, complained more, had more opinions and judgments about even the smallest things, and felt more of a need to justify my ideas to others.

That's why Infrared Level is called "Victim." We can't find

self-worth in our success, so we distract ourselves with judgments, opinions, or ideas because we need to do that to feel worthy. Or we put our heads down and work all hours, as that's the only thing we can think of doing to make ends meet. As a result, people aren't willing to give us as much time as they used to, and we don't attract the kind of opportunities we used to attract.

That's why the sole goal of Infrared Level is: Get yourself into positive territory by any means necessary. That is the only way to gain control and predictability and move to Red Level.

You may be in Infrared for the reason I was: You are not earning enough from your job to cover your living costs. You may have lost your job, you might be dealing with a huge financial setback like medical expenses or big debts, or you could simply not know what your financial situation is. People in Infrared may even look outwardly successful. Whether you are out of work or have a multimillion-dollar portfolio, if your personal cash flow is going backward every month, you are in Infrared. To build sustainable wealth, stabilizing cash flow is the first priority.

The good news is, once you commit to change, cut the distractions, and follow your genius, you can get out of Infrared in three months or less through three specific steps *dealing with your money, time, and relationships.*

The Three Steps Out of Infrared

As you will see in the stories ahead, each of the four geniuses follows the same three steps to move out of Infrared in their own natural way:

1. **Measure Your Money:** What's coming in and going out? What is your personal flow? This first step goes beyond establishing discipline over how your money flows and

extends to how your time and attention flow. For those of us who have fallen from a higher level of the lighthouse back into Infrared, this means letting go of any vestiges of that old level.

2. **Commit to Conduct:** The code by which you live each day needs to change if your habits are going to change. The key to your conduct is a commitment to reliability and consistency. The shift in conduct is from relying on yourself to solve your situation to connecting with others who are already in the flow of the markets.

3. **Do Your Duty:** Without a disciplined duty bigger than you, your slide will continue. Without forcing yourself to be accountable to make a change, nothing will change. Now is not the time to be following your passion at the expense of your discipline. Now is not the time to be saving the world. As the airline safety video says: In an emergency put on your "oxygen mask" before helping others. You'll have plenty of time for that after your oxygen is flowing and you've bought your time back!

You may understand these steps in theory—you may have even read some of them or heard them before—but remember the difference between information and direction we discussed at the start of this book: Many of us get stuck by looking at the entire map and not following the path that suits our genius. Your genius is your compass, and each of the four geniuses has a different winning formula for following these steps out of Infrared.

Following are these steps as taken by four geniuses. Regardless of your genius, read the Dynamo Genius path first to hear how my story continues and how I applied the steps that apply to all geniuses to move out of Infrared Level. Then you can skip ahead to your own genius guide—but do read all four so that you can see how the natural strategies differ.

The Dynamo Genius Path Out of Infrared

Like all Dynamo Geniuses, I found that my biggest challenge at Infrared was being overly optimistic. Dynamos are natural optimists. I was *always* saying, "It will get better tomorrow...I can always get more credit...I've still got some savings so I'll be okay...Don't worry, it will all just sort itself out."

In retrospect, saying I didn't need to worry about making $500 more to pay for my car (because I was going to be a millionaire) was like saying I didn't need to know how to swim because I was going to have a boat.

Being a Dynamo is like having an accelerator in a car—*just* the accelerator. No brake, no clutch, no gearshift. We don't like thinking small; we are always going to go for the next big thing. I tried a hundred different things, knowing I was creative and sure I could always come up with a new one.

With my Singapore publishing business, I put all the money I had into it. I was trying to accelerate my way out of trouble, but all I was really doing was revving in first gear. Even at Infrared, I would go and spend unnecessary money on some big expense in the hope it would bring more revenue. I kept taking bets I couldn't afford to lose—which, of course, meant I kept losing.

It turns out, all that was the wrong way to do it. So what did I do instead? Actually, it started with not what I did but what I *stopped* doing. The list of things not to do to get out of Infrared Level was *exactly* what I was doing. If you are a Dynamo Genius like me, here is the path to follow to take you out of Infrared:

Step One: Measure Your Money

- *Do not* invest your money and resources in your *big idea*: All resources should be directed to paying yourself first before you feed your idea, and ensuring you have positive cash flow by not investing in anything big—*yet*.

- *Do* measure your money by linking your Future Vision to the growth of your personal cash flow: Take small, steady steps by getting the support of others, and set milestones to reach before you start sprinting ahead!

Only when I put my Future Vision together did it become obvious that my family was the most important priority for me. Far more important than the business I was struggling with. I had been an embarrassment. I shared what I wrote with my wife, and she dissolved into tears. So did I. That gave us both the commitment to say "enough is enough" and create a Flight Path with very specific month-by-month quarterly milestones to make sure we as a family were going into positive cash flow—the complete opposite of me shooting for the moon.

Problem is, Dynamo Geniuses don't like being patient. They rarely enjoy the details and tracking their daily expenses. What did I do? I found a Tempo Genius who could help me go through the numbers. Now, in this case, I got lucky. My wife, Renate, is a Tempo Genius. She worked in a hospital before she became a full-time mom. So for the first time ever, I asked her to help me with my finances.

The good news is *regardless of your genius* there are always people around you who are willing to support you—your first steps in team building—provided you are willing to actually put a plan in place and be completely transparent about it.

No money? Use your family resources the way I did. Don't have a wife, family member, or good friend who is a Tempo Genius? You can trade "genius time" online, offering a creative review of a business plan written by a Tempo or Steel Genius who can help get your books in order in return. (Steel and Tempo Geniuses can offer the reverse to a Dynamo Genius for some creative input or a Blaze for some ideas on how to connect with people.) Or rent a desk in any number of the shared office spaces opening in cities all over the world where the free exchange of ideas is fueling the entrepreneurial spirit. Saying there is no one out there or you don't have the time is just an excuse. (You will find a list of the most common Infrared Level excuses later in this chapter.)

In my case, Renate and I turned money from a personal problem to a business problem as a team. We looked at the first three months and decided what it would take to organize our expenses and how much more the business would pay me. We also went to find a friend who was a Steel Genius who could help us with our accounts. We then worked out (as we will discuss shortly) how Renate could earn money using her Tempo Genius, while I worked out how the business could make more sales separately.

All this could not have been more totally opposite to what I was doing before. I had stopped trying to do it on my own and stopped my frenetic activity trying to chase business. I turned away from launching new things and took the time to work with Renate and look hard at my business so it could cover our living expenses and get us to Red Level. That was what we did in step two.

Step Two: Commit to Conduct

- *Do not* try to earn a second income by rushing in to start your own business or by focusing on your best idea—*yet*. That's not digging a new stream; it's digging a hole.
- *Do* focus on serving others who already have better, more established ideas than you do: people higher up the lighthouse who are already in flow so their flow will flow to you. Create a rhythm in your day, week, and month to keep you from burning out while serving others.

There are countless books, speakers, and TV shows that preach the value of starting your own business, but they all assume you can pay your way until you work out what works. Saying, "I'm going to start my own business, but I haven't actually figured out how to manage my own finances," is like saying, "I'm going to fly a plane without taking a flying lesson." Your chances of taking off are slim.

This is particularly true for Dynamo Geniuses who always think they will make things successful far faster than they usually do. As a result, no matter how often they make money, they find ways to spend it even faster.

So what did I do to take this second step? It was a simple shift in focus—from *expanding* what we were doing to *enhancing* what we were doing.

Once I had my small team measuring the money with a clear plan for paying me more, I set a rhythm in my day and my week that stopped the panic. I looked at how the business could simply make the extra cash flow I needed. I looked at the rates we were charging on our publications. I decided to increase our rates enough so I could increase what I paid myself while delivering an even better service to our customers. I got with the team and said, "We're going to focus on higher-paying, faster-paying customers," and they went out and found them.

Within one month I was out of Infrared. Suddenly the stress was gone. I was able to pay my bills. Now I was attracting business and people to me in a different way because I was going to work more confident. Most important, I'd bought myself my time (and my life) back.

You may say that's all easy for me to be doing, since I have a business; what if you don't have a business but are in a job? What if you're unemployed? You can't just go and say, "I'm the genius you are looking for; give me a job!" What do you do to make the extra income?

It turns out there are four gears for moving out of Infrared for any genius, depending on your assets and business/employment status (see all four at the end of the chapter). My way in my publishing business was the Yellow player path—the "second gear" way:

I already had a business, and I could use the business to deliver me the cash flow I needed.

But I also had experience with "first gear": the Foundation Prism path. This is the way to follow if you are in a job or looking for one. I know this way intimately, because *I had fallen into Infrared three years earlier, and I didn't have a business to help me get out!*

Three years before my Singapore struggles, I was living in London. I was out of my first business, seeking a second as my next "big thing," and I was trapped in Infrared with a huge tax bill from that business to pay. Of course, as a Dynamo, I was feeling optimistic that I could make things work. I had just spoken to my mentor, who gave me all kinds of good advice... which I promptly ignored. Instead, our meeting inspired me to become a consultant! I could share with other people how much I'd learned as an entrepreneur! I took all the money we had in savings (about $1,000) and put an ad in a local newspaper offering my services to support local businesses.

The ad appeared for a day and I sat by the phone waiting for it to ring. I only got one call: from a local plumber who loved my advice but was deeper in Infrared than me at that point and couldn't pay me a thing.

I remember sitting there thinking, *Maybe I'm just not cut out to be an entrepreneur.* I was desperate and losing my Dynamo hopefulness. Renate was working in a hospital to help pay the bills, but I kept assuring her I'd make money soon. Then the wake-up call came: Renate got pregnant. We were having a baby! It was one of the happiest and scariest moments of my life—and I knew it was time for me to quit "playing entrepreneur." *It was time to commit to conduct.*

I had to find a role working for someone in flow using my Dynamo Genius, or I would only be trading my time for money. I knew I was creative. I knew I could come up with good products. So, first off, I made a list of *everyone* I knew who was in flow and what he or she was up to. Then I asked: Who did *they* know who was in flow? Who could I offer my creativity to, getting paid a percentage of the results I generated?

Back then the Internet was just getting started. It fascinated me, and I went out and asked my friends who they knew in the industry that I could meet with and add value to. One thing led to another, and I found myself at the office door of a start-up set up by two senior managers at Dell, who had left with their share options and were funding an exciting new venture with Apple and Microsoft in Richmond, Surrey.

I said, "I would love to work for you guys."

They told me, "We're not hiring right now."

I said, "That's okay, just give me a week where I can just show up and help out. At the end of the week I'll give you my report on how I can help your business. Maybe there are some extra sales that could be made. Maybe there is a strategy you may be overlooking that fresh eyes will see. If you don't like anything I say, well, you've had my free labor for a week."

This is something that Dynamos do well: We can see ways to make money where money is being made. The company was intrigued by my proposal, and I got in the door. For a whole week, I shadowed the team and found ways I could help increase their sales by adding to the product range with their existing customers and reaching new customers. They liked my ideas and told me they would pay me on a percentage basis.

This is what I mean by committing to conduct: I was committed to serve someone else's business instead of just focusing on my own idea. I *knew* I wasn't looking to be a millionaire; I was looking to make the money I needed to get by.

Within a month, the company offered me a job helping with the sales, and I was out of Infrared. The next year, I became part of the senior management and thus started learning about online businesses. But I never could have made it that far if I hadn't also done the essential step three.

Step 3: Do Your Duty

- *Do not* go out and try and convince others to support you in your big idea—*yet*.
- *Do* your duty to something bigger—not you and your success.

Many people at Infrared think they already are doing their duty. I thought I was when I was at Infrared. But there is a big difference between sacrificing material things and sacrificing the very way we think for a higher level of commitment. Doing your duty is like going into the army. It's about doing something bigger than us, because if it isn't bigger than us, we will fall back into our old ways.

In both my London and Singapore stories when I was in Infrared, it took something dramatic to shift me out. Both times it was my duty to my family. In Singapore, it was my car getting repossessed and the public shame it brought on my family that led to my writing my first Future Vision. In London, Renate's pregnancy gave me renewed focus on what I wanted for my future. I was very clear with that online company from day one that the reason that I was willing to give my time and focus to them is that I believed in what they were doing. But I was also clear that I had a child on the way. I wanted to make sure I was serving my family in the right way, too.

Imagine that someone you love suddenly needs money for a medical operation: money that you don't have but need to raise. Would you force yourself to think differently and find the money? This is the nature of "Do Your Duty"—putting duty to others above your current activity and focus. I have seen people who have been stuck at the same earning level (not just Infrared) for years, having given up hope of moving higher, when suddenly their family had a need for money. They suddenly found a way to shift up.

Keep in mind that you might be in a different situation; you may have a way that you can either earn more from your current job or business or maybe add a second income stream. All that comes later. The bottom line right now is moving out of Infrared by using your genius to do so.

The issue now is *sustainability*. Doing your duty is the ultimate way any genius breaks the addiction of Infrared: making it bigger than you. But *staying* out of Infrared means *you must keep following all three steps*, not making the same mistakes all over again. After England, I didn't and fell right back into Infrared. After Singapore, I never went into Infrared again, because I had my Future Vision and stayed really clear and focused on all three steps.

That doesn't mean I did not have companies that lost money and even failed. I did. And I continue to have my fair share of ups and downs even today. But regardless of the flow of the market and my businesses, my personal plumbing system stays flowing.

Today doing my duty means I prepare each Sunday evening for the upcoming week by reading and checking in on my Future Vision, going through my Preflight Checklists, and visualizing my perfect week ahead.

The Blaze Genius Path Out of Infrared

What would I do differently in my three steps out of Infrared as a Blaze Genius? Well, I wouldn't read the books that tell me how to manage my personal finances by being an accounting whiz. Blaze Geniuses love people; there is nothing that excites them less than tracking numbers. Blaze Geniuses are similar to Dynamos in needing the process to be fun to follow, but other people distract them more than their own ideas. They're the life of any party!

Thus, while the winning formula for Blazes involves their connections and relationships, that can easily become their losing formula if the distraction leads them to chase opportunities away from what they are doing right now. If you are a Blaze Genius in Infrared, I guarantee your life is full of different opportunities you cannot decide between, and you have too many distractions stopping you from doing what you want to do. You may be busy making all those connections, but when you get home at night and look at your negative cash flow, that doesn't stop the feeling of being really alone.

These were exactly the points I made to Rustica Lamb when I began mentoring her two years ago. Rustica is a Blaze Genius who had moved from New Zealand to Bali and put her child in the same school as my children, the Green School. She had quit her job and made the move for a term. Without income, she knew this arrangement couldn't last, and she was in deep Infrared looking for a way out.

We began with her Future Vision. Rustica wanted to be involved in the growing movement in online education. In her Future Vision, she saw herself as a leader in the industry. She saw herself having a lifestyle where she could work from anywhere. She saw herself having an income that would easily cover her life in Bali and her child's education. She didn't know how all of this would happen, but she believed it would.

The biggest issue that she had was trying to set up her own business in e-learning and applying a Dynamo strategy that wasn't suited to her genius. She had struggled for years trying to start her own business, without realizing that as a Blaze Genius her flow was not in asking *what* she should do but *who* she should work with.

When I started mentoring her, I told her to turn everything around. Here's how Rustica followed her Blaze path out of Infrared.

Step One: Measure Your Money

- *Do not* ignore the money altogether; say it will take care of itself, and just follow your passion: That's what got you into trouble in the first place!

- *Do* link your Future Vision to the steady growth of your personal cash flow, and make it your top priority without getting distracted by other people and their opportunities: Gather a team to support you and make it fun.

How does a Blaze Genius measure money easily? The first step is to *not* try working out where all the money went after you spent it! There is a simple banking structure that suits a Blaze Genius, where you decide ahead of time where your money for the month needs to go. Set up automatic payments into the accounts you need for bills, cash, and contributions ahead of time, and follow a plan that doesn't rely on complicated spreadsheets. (When you are ready to set this up, all the details for doing so are in the Measure Your Money Playbook linked to your personal page on the Millionaire Master Plan website.)

Rustica immediately started measuring her money so she knew exactly how much she needed to get out of Infrared (a couple of thousand to get going). I then helped her pull together a team comprising an accountant and a friend. Rustica set her milestones with the goal of moving out of Infrared within three months. She set her weekly reviews with her team so that she would keep to her commitment.

With her new goal in front of her, it became clear that the extra cash flow she needed immediately wasn't going to happen from her e-learning start-up. That led her naturally to step two.

Step Two: Commit to Conduct

- *Do not* try and move out of Infrared by trying to start your own business *yet*—or through multiple streams of income recommended by people you've connected with—and get seduced by the variety of it all.
- *Do* seek out the friends and people you know who are in flow (or those you know who will know of others who are in flow), and work with one to grow their business through

your energy and connections in a way that is actually profitable to you!

*You've read lots of books telling you that multiple streams of income
are essential—but that's for people who are higher up the spectrum level,
already have cash flow, and have a way to support and lead their teams.*

I've heard Blazes say, "I'm going to go out and do marketing
with part of my time and trade shares with some of my time and buy
property with some of my time..." Do *not* do this. A Blaze Genius
(or any genius at Infrared) is not ready for that and shouldn't be
thinking about it. This just leads to less and less and thinner and
thinner streams of time. Stop splitting up your time and confusing
your friends without any of them actually helping you generate the
money you need.

I told Rustica to put a list together of those people she knew
in whom she placed a level of trust and who might be looking for
someone who is a people person. For a Blaze this is not difficult!

When Rustica got the word out to her network that she was
looking to make the most of her connections in New Zealand, a
contact offered her a role to help grow his recruitment company.
She took the opportunity, with the condition that she could focus
on e-learning and training. This meant she could earn an income
while building her identity. She told him she would do it on a percentage basis much as I did in England. She went one better and
negotiated for her work to be part of a new training subsidiary that
she would get ownership in if she made it a success. While I used
my Dynamo Genius to create new strategies and opportunities,
Rustica used her Blaze Genius to make connections through her
relationships and headhunting.

She moved back to New Zealand to take on the role, set up
a rhythm that kept her calm and focused, and began connecting
with the e-learning community, leading her to earn the cash flow
she needed.

Step Three: Do Your Duty

- *Do not* spend your time helping other people without getting paid, pursuing connections in the hope that one will be your next big thing, and holding on to this idea of wanting to be nice to people as the measurement of your self-worth.
- *Do* focus all your attention on doing your duty to a higher purpose that will drive you and keep you on track, whether that is your family, your friends, or the community that will ultimately benefit from your success.

Blazes want to be liked and will often get stuck and stay at Infrared as the victim because they're helping everyone else out instead of looking out for themselves first. That doesn't mean not helping your friends. It means helping in a way that is actually profitable. Set a time to connect with a team that is committed to keeping you on track every week. This may be with two others; it may be with four or five. Gather them together and appoint a leader so you can follow. You are always better when you are accountable to others. Get a Steel Genius to manage your numbers in return for your help with support and connection. Talk through the three steps and celebrate wins together.

It does not take months and months of time when you focus on the strategy like this, especially for a Blaze like Rustica. She used her genius to get out of Infrared quickly by focusing on that single stream of income in a job that suited her strengths. Don't ever think that when you go out and work for others in order to be part of their flow, it is in any way a step back from trying to start your own business. In fact, the people you work for may turn out to be the ones who support you when you launch your own business.

Most important, Rustica also did her duty by making it not all about her and what she wanted. She did what was right for her family, and that came before anything else.

Within three months of moving out of Infrared, Rustica planned the launch of an e-learning conference in New Zealand with the support of the connections she had made. She confirmed a number of well-known e-learning speakers and managed to secure the involvement of e-learning associations and groups in New Zealand. She connected the dots between established speakers and established organizations. Her senior role in the training recruitment company had given her the credibility she needed to make it happen. Just eight months after moving back to New Zealand, Rustica ran the conference successfully with a team that she had attracted. She has since launched her e-learning business, built a team that manages her recruitment division, and secured an e-learning consulting contract with a national New Zealand company.

By the end of 2013, Rustica had moved back to Bali with her family with the income, freedom, and life she imagined a year ago. She had struggled for years trying to start her own business, without realizing that as a Blaze Genius her flow was not in asking *what* she should do but *who* she should work with.

The Tempo Genius Path Out of Infrared

Speaking of family, that leads us to the Tempo path, and you already know my wife, Renate, is a Tempo Genius. You also already know the story leading up to our working as a team to get our family out of Infrared in the days after our car was towed away. I had sat down with her and explained the business's challenges and where we were. She had wanted to be part of the solution.

Then, in the same way I shared with her my Future Vision, she created her own, as she had her own dreams and her own path to follow. Remember: Tempo is the opposite of Dynamo. Her strengths would be my weaknesses and vice versa: While Dynamos have their heads in the clouds, Tempos have their feet on the ground. The only way for me to fly like a kite was to have Renate hold the string!

Tempos take longer to make decisions and to let go of the things they have gotten used to. While Dynamos are quicker to make money (and quicker to spend it), Tempos don't have a to-do list of new ideas in the same way and often struggle to work out how to make money. The strength of Tempo Geniuses is that they are not as quick to spend as Dynamo and Blaze Geniuses and are more careful with how money flows out. Their challenge is working out how to increase the flow in.

Step One: Measure Your Money

- *Do not* just jump into some moneymaking activity because it has been recommended to you by a friend or try to follow a system to make money faster, like share trading, property investing, or online marketing—*yet*.
- *Do* turn your budgeting into a forward forecast linked to your Future Vision, and then work with a team that will help guide you to the easiest, most certain way to generate the extra cash you need in your plan to move out of Infrared!

Tempos know they're not going to create something new like Dynamos, but they have a great sense of timing and thus can get seduced by someone selling something. That is not where Tempo money should be going at this point. It locks it up in a way that leaves you without the cash flow you need; you end up asset rich and cash poor.

Tempos should bring onto their team a Dynamo or Blaze Genius who will be able to help direct them to the simplest way to earn. At our first little team meeting, Renate said she wanted to be earning, but how? We went through different possibilities: A job at a hospital? The hours wouldn't work. A management job? Not much fun. Something in property? Now, that was something that interested her. We had narrowed down to an industry she was interested in, and that's when we moved to step two.

Step Two: Commit to Conduct

- *Do not* spend all your time being busy, getting a false sense of achievement by having your hands full with activity that is not earning you the money you need.
- *Do* direct all your efforts toward a role where you are being profitably rewarded for bringing your natural strengths of reliability and service to a team in flow, with the help of your most creative or connected friends.

Tempos are at their best when in the midst of activity, but this works against them in Infrared. Tempo is all about reliable service, care, and action. Renate was so busy being busy every day, there was no time to sit down and commit to connect and *focus* and then go out there and earn money.

Tempos do not have the same risk appetite as a Dynamo and will only start moving when they have gained a comfort level with what they are doing and the best way to do it. By working together with a Dynamo Genius, Tempos can get the direction they need. Knowing she was interested in property—and knowing that this was *not* the time to put our own money into property investments—I worked with Renate on options to get involved in the property market that would generate income.

As a Tempo Genius (and a new mom), Renate had many close friends in Singapore. They were all renting property, and most would move every two years. How easy would it be to help them find their new home as a property agent? We worked out she would only need four successful rentals in the year to reach the cash flow target she had set to help us move out of Infrared.

I connected Renate with one of our biggest clients in our property magazine, Dennis Wee, a property agency with a great training program for agents. Renate was welcomed with open arms into their program. She set a rhythm that worked for herself and the family, and that gave her the time to go through the training and get set up as an agent.

The result? She reached and then exceeded her own targets within six months, and she became so successful we set up a new company, Expat Rentals, to serve the expat market in Singapore. Today it's one of the leading expat rental firms in the country.

Step Three: Do Your Duty

- *Do not* close off the rest of the world and retreat into your own activity.
- *Do* get connected by gathering a support team that can help you focus on a path that commits to a higher duty.

Tempos are not extroverted like Blazes. They will spend more time alone—which means they'll spend more time without support. If you are a Tempo Genius, you can manage spreadsheets and are most likely counting your costs already. You don't need a group like Blaze Geniuses to make things happen, but you do need a team to keep you focused and reassure you about the tough decisions you need to make.

As with Dynamo and Blaze Geniuses, Tempos need a cause bigger than themselves to move out of Infrared. All of us can bear the pain of being in Infrared on our own, but we cannot bear seeing others suffering from our actions. For Renate and me, working together by being honest about our situation was critical to getting out and staying out of Infrared. Many times it is your family or close friends who will help support you—but make sure they or *anyone* you are seeking support from are in flow and connected.

It is no coincidence that there are so many comeback stories in which only a time of real hardship allowed people to get real. The habits we set then, and the systems we put in place, are the same ones Renate and I use today. By doing her duty, Renate sowed the seeds that led to her realizing not just her dreams but my dream as well: The property experience she gained in Singapore has led to us growing a property portfolio around the world—including buying our resort in Bali!

The Steel Genius Path Out of Infrared

Flow was far from where another married couple was when I met them in 2011. Lisa and Lachlan Laing had begun a business selling solar-powered heaters in Australia. Times had been tough, and they had fallen into Infrared as they put all their money into managing their business. Like Renate and me, the stress of it had affected their personal relationship as well. For the sake of their marriage, they were questioning whether they should still be working together—or if they even still had the motivation to manage the business.

In their case, Lachlan is a Steel Genius and Lisa is a Dynamo Genius. They had just had a baby, and cautious Steel Lachlan was taking a traditional I-can-make-the-decisions-here approach, while Dynamo Lisa was saying, "Okay, so, *what are we doing?*"

But Steel Lachlan had no way to give Lisa's creative, future-thinking Dynamo that kind of answer. He was pessimistic about the industry and the future of their business and at the same time stubbornly resistant to change. He would say something like, "We're going to keep on making a go of it." And she would respond, "Okay...but then why don't we do this or that?" And then he would tell her to "stop second-guessing" him.

That's how I first met them. It had gotten to a point where they knew things needed to change. We began with their Future Vision. It quickly became obvious to both of them that they *would* rather work together if they could work things out, and they both had dreams of a new business making a difference in the world—they just didn't know what yet. Here are the three steps Lachlan, using his Steel Genius, used to move with Lisa out of Infrared.

Step One: Measure Your Money

- *Do not* spend your time being judgmental and critical of how others are doing things and use this as a reason for inaction.
- *Do* focus your analytical skills on a financial plan that links to your Future Vision and that inspires a team to work with you on solutions to achieve the plan.

Steel Geniuses are the most deep thinking and analytical of the four geniuses. They will see the three steps to get out of Infrared as common sense—but still find it incredibly hard to get their heads around what to do. That's because Steel Geniuses always feel there is a better way to do things and are forever seeing the risks and downside.

Steels at Infrared have *no* problem saving money. They have a problem making *more* money. Dynamo and Blaze Geniuses are naturally good at making money, because they connect the ideas and the people. But they are not so good at keeping the money. Tempo and Steel Geniuses are brilliant at being able to keep the money and calculating exactly where it all is, but they are not so good at putting their foot on the accelerator.

Like Lachlan, Steel Geniuses in Infrared usually have spread-sheets and budgets in place, but they hold on to cash-draining assets or low-paying jobs and find it hard to make a decision, especially as they are so fearful of even greater losses. What Steels need to do is connect with the people who know how to do that. The value Steels bring to the table is in cutting costs. (If this is you, perhaps you can get a percentage of the return if you help others make more profit rather than more sales, as I did as a Dynamo.)

In Lachlan's case, all he had to do was look across the dinner table to see the Dynamo he needed to connect with. He and Lisa put together a team and a financial plan to move out of Infrared. There was a big shift in their cash flow that they needed to follow, and they didn't know how they would do it. But by having the plan, they could then commit to conduct.

Step Two: Commit to Conduct

- *Do not* spend all your time on the details, trying to get ahead through analysis and attempting to grow things on your own.
- *Do* work with the help of others to find the flow, create a rhythm with a team to keep you on track and positive, and trade your ability to be detail- and system-focused with those who can open the flow up to you.

Steel Geniuses have their foot on the brake instead of the accelerator. They internalize—they want to get things perfect before they move forward. When Lachlan and Lisa found out they were Steel and Dynamo Geniuses, it suddenly made sense to them how they could work together (and where their frustrations had come from).

First they created a rhythm where they would spend 80 percent of their time working to achieve their cash flow targets on their existing business and 20 percent dreaming on their new business. Lisa focused on ways to increase revenues with a series of promotions, and Lachlan negotiated increased payment terms with their suppliers. They changed their priority from trying to grow the business further to increasing its efficiency and quality.

The result? They cut salary costs by reducing the size of the team, and they cut marketing costs by increasing referrals. With revenues unchanged, they made the extra money they needed to pay themselves what they needed to move out of Infrared, and this gave them the breathing space to plan the future.

Step Three: Do Your Duty

- *Do not* cut yourself off from those around you while you try to work things out.
- *Do* find someone—*anyone*—to be accountable to: Hold yourself to a bigger cause with a dynamic leader or people person to work with to get you back into flow.

Steel Geniuses want to do things on their own and isolate themselves when they're at Infrared Level with no idea how to turn the cash flow back on. At Infrared Level, Tempo and Blaze get lost in either people or activity, while Dynamo and Steel always try to do it on their own, but when Steels like Lachlan (or Dynamos like me) do that, they cut themselves off from the very help they need.

I worked with Lachlan and Lisa on their Future Vision—a picture of an inspiring perfect life a year in the future with all their troubles behind them and extra money in the bank. I asked them what they would be doing and what would be different. Of course they would still be working together. They would also be in business supporting the environment, but it would be a business with more heart, supporting families.

We then created a rhythm for each week and each day that would allow them to get there, and I shared with them how I begin every day with eight questions that ensure every day begins stress-free. (You can find these eight questions at the end of the book.) Having a path that their business served, instead of them feeling like slaves to the business, empowered and united them. It made the hard decisions they were making in their business easier.

Within months they had decided on their new business. Lisa had a long list of ideas, and together we narrowed it down to Eco-riginals, a company that serves environmentally conscious families with the first fully eco-diapers in Australia. "Doing Their Duty" to Lachlan and Lisa became more than just accountability to their family: They now had a mission to serve families all over the country. They attracted thousands of fans and pre-orders in advance of the launch, with the first container-load shipping in to Australia less than two years after we first met.

Does this mean that by moving out of Infrared, we all live happily ever after? No! The journey continues! Lachlan and Lisa, just like Renate and me, continue to have good times and tough times. We're all human. But rising up the lighthouse is like sailing out to sea. The waves get bigger. Your successes and challenges get bigger. But with more flow—like wind in the sails—you can navigate these waves a little more easily, and when you need the time or money to support your journey, it's there.

The Four Gears to Move Out of Infrared

Much as in the process of improving your health, until you know what's happening with your own wealth flow, you can't begin to improve it. Being in Infrared is like having a leaky plumbing system. No matter how much money you earn, it always disappears. Measuring your money is all about fixing those leaks and turning your cash-flow plan into a million-dollar plumbing system.

Try this exercise with me: You have two weeks to go out and earn money by whatever means possible—money that will increase your own personal cash flow. You can go out and find an hourly job. You can do something with your business. You can moonlight. You decide how you're going to make the money.

Thinking about these two weeks and all the possibilities available to you, what are you confident you could make? Could you make $10? Could you make $100? We'll keep adding a zero until you're not so confident anymore. Could you make $1,000? How about $10,000? $100,000?

When I did this exercise with a group recently, only half the hands stayed up at $1,000, and only a few after that. Everyone could make it to $100. Yet *no one* was focusing on that $100. It's not that we dismiss $100; it's just that most of us cannot be bothered with $100 because we want to go out and make a million dollars. *But the real key is not learning how to become a millionaire.* The real key is discovering, if you know how to make $100, how can you stretch it to $1,000? That's what you need to set up now: a way to make $1,000. Would an extra $500 a week cover your basic living expenses and get you to even cash flow and the Red Survivor Level? For most of us at Infrared Level, it would, or it isn't far off.

That's why, regardless of your genius, every single path out of Infrared starts with answering the question: *What is the actual amount of money I need so that I am no longer cash negative every month?*

For some people it is as little as a couple hundred dollars. For others it may be several thousand. But knowing that number is the very first step toward moving from Infrared to Red. That's how we stay focused on moving out of negative personal cash flow as fast as possible and thus moving out of stress as fast as possible.

So what is that number for you?

Once you know that number, ask yourself: *Is there any way to close the gap between that number and what I have now by cutting down some of my expenses?* (Not forever—just to get to Red Level.) That's a critical step that *buys you your time* and allows you to move forward and see things differently, without the same level of stress and anxiety. How quickly could you make that happen?

Once you know what that amount is and you have brought down your costs to a level where you can just cover that gap, you can better see how each person in these Infrared stories found a way to cover that gap. There are four main ways—like four gears in a car—to move out of Infrared. The gear you choose depends on your circumstances before you fell into Infrared. They connect to the levels from Orange to Blue—all of which link to market flow:

Orange Level Strategy (Gear One): Take this gear if you don't have a business, a team, or cash-draining assets you can sell. Cut your costs and get a job that pays you what you need to move out of Infrared. That does not mean just throwing yourself into the job market. It also doesn't mean having to get a job you don't enjoy or that pays you too little. In chapter 4, I will tell you how to find the right job for your genius and passion, and how to choose your team instead of waiting for a team to choose you. (This is the gear Rustica and Renate took.)

Yellow Level Strategy (Gear Two): If you are self-employed or a small-business owner working at Yellow Level, you will know how to run promotions that deliver revenue and profit to your business. You can run a promotion that delivers enough direct income into your personal pocket to move you out of Infrared. Focus on what generates the greatest cash flow to move out, and you can move out rapidly. (This is the gear I took, as did Lachlan and Lisa.)

Green Level Strategy (Gear Three): If you already own a business as a Green Performer and know how to redirect your teams to generate extra cash flow that ends up in your pocket, some swift changes can result in you getting out of Infrared quickly. It could be as basic as paying yourself more from the business instead of leaving it in there. Simple as this sounds, do it, and you will immediately feel a positive shift in your energy when you see the positive result in your bank account.

Blue Level Strategy (Gear Four): If you are sitting on multiple assets or debt, moving out of Infrared can simply be a matter of reorganizing your assets and debt. That means selling properties that are costing you money every month and closing down the businesses that are burning a hole in your personal pocket. It is the time to reorganize your interest payments and how you pay back the debt. Not to pay it all off but simply to go cash flow positive every month. Now is not the time to hope for your asset values to increase or to get nostalgic about your business or house.

Choose your strategy and then start following the steps and the actions out of Infrared and move to Red and beyond. If for any reason you are stuck and don't even know how you would make an extra $500 or $1,000, *don't worry*! In the next chapter I will give you a step-by-step exercise that lets you identify and connect with the right people who can be directing their flow to you. For now, focus on the smallest amount possible to improve your cash flow, take the following steps to measure your money, and set your plan and schedule. Commit to *what* and *when* first; *who* and *how* will follow.

By the way, if you are reading this chapter and you are already in positive cash flow, work through those three steps anyway so that you have a strong foundation to ensure that you stay out of Infrared. It is all too easy to stop tracking your own personal finances as you become more successful.

This is the one strategy that I would credit for my personal wealth (and why it is the first step for each genius): measuring my money and increasing the net cash flow I have every three months when I was at Infrared Level. Your first step is simply to measure what you need in order to get out of Infrared. The key steps for mapping out your personal income are in the Measure Your Money Playbook on your Millionaire Master Plan website page.

What you want to create for the first time here, as you move from Infrared to Red, is a rhythm for how you measure and grow your wealth—starting with the first extra dollar—that can last you through to the time when there are millions flowing through your accounts each year.

So Stop Making Excuses; Start Being a Survivor!

You remember I said we are all geniuses. So why do so many of us get stuck in negative cash flow? Well, we are all geniuses at doing certain things, and we are even bigger geniuses at coming up with excuses for *not* doing things. Here are the Top 5 Excuses that create resistance to our flow and keep us at Infrared Level:

1. **I can't cut back my costs:** If you are in a job with a steady income and you are in Infrared, you are overspending. Truth is, there are *always* people earning less than you who have worked out ways to stay cash positive. There is *always* a way to cut back costs.

2. **I can't earn more than I'm earning:** Whether you are employed or self-employed, you get to design how much you earn. It isn't about how talented you are or how hard you work; it is about what value you are delivering and who you are delivering it to.

3. **I'll be out soon:** Many people know they are in Infrared, but rather than putting together a proper plan to get out, they fantasize about winning the lottery or making their business super-successful. (That was me as my car was towed away.) Instead it's the small, sure-thing actions you take that guarantee you move out.

4. **I need to follow my passion:** You may have read books telling you to follow your passion. Good advice, unless you are in Infrared. If you want to go on a diet and simply follow your passion—eating chocolate cake—you clearly haven't found the solution. In fact, this is what got you in trouble in the first place. You need to put discipline before passion.

5. **My investments need the money more than me:** There are a surprising number of people who are asset rich and cash

poor. Perhaps you have bought properties and other investments over the years. The problem is that they are costing
you money to keep, because they are in negative cash flow.
Simply selling your negative cash flow investments could
turn you positive. It's the pain of letting go that stops you
from doing it. Get into the flow and let it go.

I have made every single one of these excuses at one point in
my life—some many, many times. I have also made all the mistakes everyone makes to fall back into or get stuck in Infrared.

I have insisted on doing it myself: Infrared comes from
disconnection. Trying to "prove yourself" by starting a
business or getting others interested in helping you instead
of you being interested in helping them is a sure formula for
failure, leaving you stuck at this level.

I have blamed others: The easiest way to cope with the anxiety
of Infrared is to blame others. It may help us feel better, but it
doesn't change our situation. In fact, it stops us from taking
full responsibility and control of our lives, which is what we
need to do before we can change. It also stops us from being
attractive to the people who can help us get into flow, and
it attracts others who also want to blame and complain—
which means we surround ourselves with people who are
also Infrared, making it doubly difficult to move out.

I have picked fights: Fighting those whom you blame may
feel productive and satisfying for the temporary release
it brings, but directing all your negative energy into such
fights is usually ineffective. If you really feel strongly about
something, get into power and change it from the inside.
Anything else is just a distraction to keep you at Infrared,
where you're left with the negativity or frustration you've
attracted.

And if you have done any of these things or made any of these excuses—or even if you are just stuck and on the verge of losing hope—there is one last thing before we move on to the Red Survivor and Orange Worker Levels: **It is going to be okay.**

Sure, if someone had told me this when I was standing on the street in Singapore, I would not have believed it, but I've made it my life's purpose to absolutely make sure that you *do* get out of it. World Wide Wealth is not about a *few* people creating more and contributing more wealth. It is about *all* of us being able to do that collectively. Maybe you think you have read every book that there is to read about doing this. You've read about cleaning up your credit cards and managing your money and still find it challenging to do. You have lost belief in yourself. Well, there are others who believe in you, and there will be *many* who will be thanking you when you are earning and giving at your full potential.

Not only is it still going to be okay, but here's another thing to remember: **You can't blame yourself for it.** Every genius falls into a shadow when that genius is extinguished. If Dynamos aren't given the opportunity to create and instead are made to work on their weaknesses, they will lose all confidence in their ability to add value in the world. Same for Blazes who aren't given the chance to work with people and are forced to focus on detail, Tempos who aren't able to serve others and must come up with new ideas all the time, and Steels who aren't given a chance to complete things well and have to spend their time in front of people. When the shadow consumes our genius, we don't do any of the stuff that makes up our natural strengths.

The way you can move out is by following the stories of others like the ones here. Through them, you will feel what it's like to move out of this level, too. That's why when you move out of Infrared, you may simply move to Red Level, but some people jump straight to Yellow, Green, or Blue Level. That is because some people who already know how to run a business, be part of a high-performing team, or invest in a portfolio simply need to reorganize their personal finances to move out of Infrared.

So it is going to be okay—you are worth more than this.

It is going to be okay.

You are worth more than this.

CHAPTER THREE SUMMARY

- Infrared Level is a world of static and stress.
- Infrared Level is negative cash flow: You can have millions in assets and still be Infrared—moving out must be your first priority.
- You can move out of Infrared by following these three steps:

  Measure Your Money
  Commit to Conduct
  Do Your Duty

- Every genius has a different strategy for these three steps that involves *doing* new things and *not doing* the other things that got them into Infrared in the first place.
- There are four gears for getting out of Infrared, ranging from Orange to Blue Level.
- There are three steps to stay in Infrared: Trying to do it yourself, blaming others for your situation, and picking a fight (focusing on the negative).
- Excuses also keep us trapped at this level: *I can't cut back my costs, I can't earn more than I'm earning, I'll be out soon, I need to follow my passion*, and *My investments need the money more than me.*
- Remember: It is going to be okay. Just follow the steps.

Preflight Checklist: Red Level

Before getting busy with business, you must know what your personal financial milestones are, ensuring you are growing a positive net flow each month. Your personal page on www.millionairemasterplan.com has supplemental guides and videos, including assessments and Playbooks, for each of the checklist points below. I have included one of the exercises from the Playbook at the end of this chapter: how to design your spaces to suit your genius.

Complete the checklist now: Tick yes or no. How do you rate? When all nine are checked yes, you will have built the plumbing system you need to stay well and truly out of Infrared Level.

Measure Your Money

1. I have a system to measure my personal finances every month and know what my monthly net income is. ☐ Yes ☐ No

2. I have a simple monthly forecast and actuals for my personal finances that allow me to track my progress. ☐ Yes ☐ No

3. I have a banking system and review system to ensure I am always aware of my personal financial position. ☐ Yes ☐ No

Commit to Conduct

1. I have designed my relationships, environment, spaces, and travel to keep me in flow and at my best. ☐ Yes ☐ No

2. I follow a rhythm to plan my time and activities every year, month, and week that keeps me balanced and inspired. ☐ Yes ☐ No

3. I have a daily rhythm that energizes me in mind, body, and spirit, and keeps me in good health and vitality. ☐ Yes ☐ No

Do Your Duty

1. I consider the actions that align to my Flight Path as my first priority, and I commit to these actions daily.   ☐ Yes   ☐ No

2. I am disciplined in managing my distractions and emotions, and I am surrounded by people who support my path.   ☐ Yes   ☐ No

3. I ensure I seek out answers and support, and I have the courage to act in the face of uncertainty.   ☐ Yes   ☐ No

ACTION POINT

Design Your Spaces to Suit Your Geniuses

WHY?
Spirit

Reflection
& Renewal

HOW?
Steel

Details &
Financials

WHAT?
Dynamo

Creation &
Planning

WHEN?
Tempo

Service &
Schedule

WHO?
Blaze

Meeting &
Connecting

A key to measuring your money at every level is to create a rhythm to manage your time and money that is aligned to your genius; energizes, engages, and keeps you in flow; and assigns value to the spaces of other geniuses.

We all have a bit of every genius in us, but we have one predominant genius that is our path to success. For my Dynamo Genius, my path is using my creativity, but following that path does not excuse me for inexcusable behavior when it comes to the other geniuses inside me. In other words, a Dynamo like me can't say, "Well, I am creative so I don't have to do anything but create. I do not need to speak to anyone or worry about numbers." Yes, I do.

I am at Blue Level of the Wealth Lighthouse today, and I know this more than ever. I know that if I don't set aside a little bit of Steel time with my finance team every week and month, then I am going to miss something somewhere and lose the rhythm I have created. When I step into my "Steel" space, I become "Steel Roger." While this is not my natural genius, I can tap into the smaller Steel Genius in me, with high standards in my attention to detail and low tolerance for madcap thinking. I only need an hour, and in that hour, I understand where the numbers are in all my businesses everywhere—because the hour is set up that way.

Now, you have most likely tried some time management techniques, and one may still be working for you. One of the biggest problems I encounter, however, is people who constantly try to squeeze too much activity into too little time.

The trick to shift this is to realize it isn't just *when* you do things, it's *where* you do them. Our environment is a much bigger factor in our lives than we realize. Too many of us have created stress and are overwhelmed in our lives by mixing up our energies. Sitting at a desk to try to study your finances, getting interrupted by phone calls, and then going back to your spreadsheet is like trying to freeze ice and boil water all in the same place. An enormous amount of energy is spent simply trying to switch from one state to another. Of course this is going to cause stress.

At my resort in Bali, I have designed five different pavilions that create five different types of energy. Depending on whether I have creative activities, where I am adding the *What?*; or people to speak to, where I am connecting the *Who?*; or plans to review (*When?*); or data to analyze (*How?*); or my vision to reflect on (*Why?*), I set times of each week and each day when I will physically move into the best space for the energy I need.

Take the time now to design your week using the five frequencies we discussed in chapter 1 (aligned to the four geniuses and the fifth "spirit" frequency that unites them all), then decide on the place and time to do each and stick to it. Place your natural genius frequency as your Wednesday, so it anchors your week, and then flow from there. So, for example, if you are a Dynamo Genius, make Wednesday your Dynamo Day, then Thursday your Blaze Day, and so on. Here is how it works for me:

Dynamo Space: This is your space to brainstorm, write creatively, come up with new ideas, and answer the question, *What?* Make it a place where you can pin things up and see the big picture. Don't take phone calls here or text-message or use any kind of social media. Don't get stuck in details or distracted by others.

Blaze Space: This is your space to have conversations, answer emails, take phone calls, and answer the question, *Who?* When you step into this space, you will have everyone's contact information close at hand, photos of people who are important, and Post-it notes of conversations and threads to follow. Make this a space of conversation, where there is no room to daydream or procrastinate.

Tempo Space: This is your space to be calm and grounded and to sit with team members to plan or with clients to listen. This is where everything has a *When?* and *Where?* This isn't a place to promote or sell, but a place to provide care and service and take care of smaller people-related activities. Don't let any overly positive or overly negative energy into this space.

Steel Space: This space allows you to concentrate on the detail, get quiet time, and focus clearly on the *How?* This is where you keep all your finances and spreadsheets and where all your detailed files can be easily accessed. Keep out all interruptions, and have no phones, emails, or distractions in this space. Be willing to be critical and to take criticism from here.

Spirit Space: This space inspires you and allows you to reflect on your higher purpose and bigger mission. This is where you get to breathe and bring out your inner smile. Every morning I begin in my spirit space and ask myself eight questions to begin every day (see the Action Point following chapter 8).

What are the productive environments that you can create to redesign the standards you set for your mind, body, and spirit each day? Even if you have a full-time job or have your hands full with children, there is always a way to reorganize your time and space to bring out your best self. Once you have your spaces, design your schedule and keep to it. Hold yourself to a standard by which you aren't late to a space because you became caught up in the space before. Just as I won't want to make someone wait for me because I'm late for an appointment, I won't make my Blaze Roger wait for me because my Dynamo Roger is hogging my time!

FROM RED TO ORANGE: SURVIVOR TO WORKER

Measure:	Zero—no shortfall or surplus cash flow every month
Emotions:	Anxiety; stress; relief
Cost of staying here:	Exhaustion; resignation; life repeating itself
Focus needed:	Passion and connection
How did I get here?	Impatience; distraction; conditioning
How do I move up?	Pinpoint Your Passion; Set Your Standards; Follow the Flow

R ed Level may be only one level from the bottom, but it feels a whole lot different from Infrared up here. In my own life, every time I went from Infrared to Red, I had an overwhelming sense of relief from just being able to pay all the bills at the end of the month. I stopped feeling so anxious and uncertain and started having some self-worth. I gave myself permission to enjoy life again. I connected with others in a positive way and no longer felt the same compelling urge to voice my opinion, complain, or criticize.

All these feelings were good, but in my earlier days, they also came with temptation to let my Dynamo Genius run wild again. Now that I was not losing money, I started to think about the other products and services I could create to make money faster...and wound up back in Infrared.

That's why these good feelings at Red come with a choice: *Keep climbing the ladder to wealth or try to get to wealth by jumping on a trampoline, always coming back to Red—or even falling off, back to Infrared.*

Just Enough Money to Have Nothing

You may be at Red Level because your world is revolving around your job or business more than it is revolving around your personal wealth and well-being. You may be here because you have always been in the habit of spending what you make, or you've organized your investments so the money stays in them and you never get to savor their flow. You might be here because your parents or spouse are supporting you. Or maybe you are in a lower-paying job and don't know how to find something that earns you more.

Regardless of your circumstances or age, how successful your business is, or why you are at Red Level, you are a "Survivor," because any extra money gets spent on survival instead of invested or keeping up appearances and showing others that you can afford things (even if you can't).

You're not drowning anymore, but you are still treading water. The plumbing has flow, the tap is on, but there's no plug. You have just enough to afford your bills, perhaps a few luxuries or a little extra pay; it is not going toward growing your personal wealth as much as giving you permission to distract yourself. As a result, you feel like you can "go for the win" by investing in some stocks, property, or big ideas—but no matter how many times you try doing that at this level: *You come right back to zero.*

There is nothing wrong with trying to invest in your ideas, business, stocks, or property, but it is not sustainable at Red Level. Living week-to-week, all decisions are short-term. And that can lead to a sense of frustration and helplessness about not being able to move up farther.

That's why the feelings at Red Level are of relief *and* resignation. As I mentioned, staying here is like being on a trampoline. You may bounce higher—perhaps even very high—but you never stay up; you always fall back to where you started. To get to Orange Level and beyond—to truly *build* wealth—you can't bounce; you need to climb. To do that, you need what every builder needs: the steps of a ladder.

In fact, there are only Ten Steps to a Million Dollars from here. I know; I took them. Using your genius, you can take the ten steps up the Wealth Lighthouse. Now that you are out of Infrared Level, you are out of the basement of the lighthouse, and the first of the ten steps can begin.

The Ten Steps to a Million

To my embarrassment, the plan I used to get out of Infrared after I watched my car being towed away in Singapore was a plan that a mentor of mine, a millionaire, had given me *years* earlier when I asked him questions about my business. *I just didn't listen to him because I thought I knew better.*

At the time, I was living in London and had a publishing business that was still struggling to make money. I had a chance to meet my first *real* millionaire! I remember speaking to him excitedly about my business, asking him questions I had written down about our product strategy, how to set up partnerships, and whether I was hiring the right people.

"How long have you been losing money?" he asked me, interrupting my enthusiastic run of questions.

"Oh, the business is still in its first three years," I replied, trying to explain the lack of profit.

"No. I'm not talking about the business. I'm talking about you. How long have you personally been losing money?"

How did he know I was losing money? This was before Singapore, before I understood anything about this Millionaire Master Plan, so I didn't realize how much my Infrared heat was radiating. "What do you mean?" I asked, clueless.

"How much do you put aside each month into your investment portfolio?"

"Ah! No, I don't have an investment portfolio," I said, laughing. "I'm not an investor. I'm an entrepreneur. I put all my money in my business."

He just shook his head. "If you want any advice from me, come back when you have positive cash flow and an investment portfolio. I can't invest time with you if you're not willing to invest in yourself." With those words, he began to leave.

"Wait!" I cried out. "Don't go. I'm sorry. I didn't mean to upset you," I said in confusion. "I would really value your help. What are you saying I should do?"

He stopped and sat down again. "The reason you can't make your business cash positive is because you're not even making yourself cash positive. If you're serious about building some wealth and being of value, begin with yourself."

"I'm a fast learner," I said, folding away my list of questions. "What do you want me to do?"

"Just get to the end of a month with $100 more than you had the month before." He smiled. "Just pay yourself $100 more than you spend. Simple."

I looked at him with a half frown, careful not to upset him again. "I could do that now. I just need to spend a bit less each week."

"Great!" he said.

I paused. That was it? "What then?" I asked.

"Then, double it. Put aside $200. Once you've done that, double it again."

"To $400?" I asked. He nodded. "In the third month?" I asked.

"If you like; the time frame is up to you," he replied.

"How is saving $400 going to make me wealthy or help my business?"

"Ask me that again after you're worked out what happens once you double the number ten times."

So, I wrote it out:

- $200
- $400
- $800
- $1,600
- $3,200
- $6,400
- $12,800
- $25,600
- $51,200
- $102,400

If $102,400 was my monthly net cash flow every month, I would have an annual million-dollar income after ten months with two months in the year to spare. A million dollars in cash flow every year by simply growing my monthly net cash flow.

Still, that seemed unfathomable to me. I couldn't see getting past step four. I shook my head. "I understand how I would get to maybe $800 or even $1,600 extra every month by working hard and generating more sales and paying myself more from that. But I can't believe I will ever work out how to double from $25,000 to $50,000 in one month, especially if that's just ten months from now!"

"First of all," he said, "you will find it's easier to move up the higher you go. Second, you don't need to increase every month. What if you were to double every year? Do you think you could work out how to get from $50,000 to $100,000 a month if that was ten years from now?"

I thought about that. I was twenty-two, and being thirty-two seemed so far in the future—and so old! "Oh no!" I said. "I definitely could do it faster than that."

"So, monthly is too fast. Yearly is too slow. We're not arguing about whether you can get to a million anymore. *We're just arguing about when.*"

I remember leaving that meeting energized and then forgetting the conversation until the day my car was repossessed. Part of the plan I created that fateful night was to finally commit to my mentor's ten-step strategy. I figured that if I doubled my personal net income every three months, I could get through all ten steps in two and a half years. Either it would work, or it would be a thirty-month experiment that failed.

We all have the opportunity to begin to do this at Red Level. It simply involves choosing between expanding and enhancing what we are doing.

I had spent my life trying to expand—to make my business bigger—as opposed to enhancing what was there and make it better. The difference is that when I was expanding, I was growing revenue but not profit. When I was enhancing, I was focusing on the things I already had and asking, "How can I make it more profitable? How can I make more from my best customers? How can I do this process better or make some little tweaks this way and that to pay myself a few extra dollars a week?"

What happened to me next and how I climbed the ladder is detailed in the Dynamo Genius path that follows in this chapter and those to come, but the short answer is I made a shift in my pay every three months and kept finding new ways to stretch what I earned. Six months later, I had taken my first two steps to a million and gotten all the way to the $400 net cash flow a month by just making sure my company was focusing on making a profit rather than growing.

I went positive, then even more positive, and as my income increased, I started to look for more opportunities. By the second year, I was already feeling very differently about money. I then raised venture capital and expanded. I invested in property that would give me a high cash return. My flow kept growing, and with it my thinking grew. It took me about three years to get to a million dollars in cash flow, but I got there. And I credit my mentor's ten-step mind-set for moving me out of Infrared into Red Level and up the Wealth Lighthouse.

So how many months will it take you to get to $100 net positive cash flow and then double it to start to move up from Red Level and take the first step to a million? Once you have that answer, follow these three Red Level steps to get off the trampoline and start climbing your way to Orange and beyond.

Three Steps to Move From Red to Orange

At every level in the Wealth Lighthouse, the four geniuses follow the same three steps to move out of Red in their own natural way. But these are *not* the same steps as Infrared or any level.

At the end of chapter 2, I showed how we move up the Wealth Lighthouse in a pattern that zigzags from *drivers*, who have the freedom of choice to drive their vehicles but not build them, to *designers*, who have the freedom of movement to build their vehicles but not drive them everywhere they want to go. At Red Level, you are a designer. Thus moving to Orange Level demands a different winning formula than you used at Infrared Level: Instead of starting by focusing outside (on your connection with others), you need to focus inside (on your connection to yourself). Instead of tapping into your discipline and commitment, you are tapping into your passion and purpose:

1. **Pinpoint Your Passion:** The only reason you are on the Red Level trampoline is that you have no motivation to stop bouncing and start climbing. The turning point comes when you reconnect to the things that light you up—with a job or role in your enterprise aligned with your passions. (My friends Janet and Chris Attwood created the Passion Test, which you can use to find your passions. Find a link to it on your personal page on www.millionairemasterplan.com.)

2. **Set Your Standards:** This is like the "Commit to Conduct" in Infrared, only it's about quality not discipline. No one ever became a millionaire sustainably with sloppy standards. What are the standards you can raise in your thoughts and action? How you are spending your time? Who are you connecting with? How can you raise your standards from how you spend your time to how you invest your time? What will you no longer settle for?

3. **Follow the Flow:** The biggest mistake people make when trying to move forward (and then end up staying at Red Level or falling back to Infrared) is trying to do it on their own. There is already plenty of flow in the world, with money, value, and knowledge changing hands every day. You need to tap that flow by seeking out others already in it, attracting them, and getting their money flowing to, and aligned with, your passion.

The following examples detail these steps as taken by each of the four geniuses. Regardless of your genius, read the Dynamo Genius path first to hear how my story continues, and then read your genius's path. But do read all four so that you can see how the winning and losing formulas differ for each.

Then be sure to read the concluding lessons on using your Superman Time and the language of flow. These will set you up for success as you move from Red to Orange and beyond.

The Dynamo Genius Path Out of Red

Picking up where my story left off in my Ten Steps to a Million, I had managed to move from $0 extra put aside each month to $800 by enhancing my small publishing business. I found better-paying clients and created new sections in my property magazine for new markets like home furnishing and property services. But I had gotten to the point where enhancing the business model was not going to get me to the next steps of $800 and $1,600 extra per month. I knew I needed to make money in different ways, and *that meant confronting the things that stopped me from going forward in the first place.*

Step One: Pinpoint Your Passion
- *Do not* go chasing the next big thing and overextend yourself, relying only on your own Dynamo Genius for your next best idea.
- *Do* use your freedom of movement to take the time to look for people who share the same passion as you, who you would love to be working with, and who are already in profitable flow—for every person who has time and no money, there is someone else who has money and no time.

When we feel the relief of being at Red Level, all Dynamos have a tendency to put our foot back on the pedal and try to expand and grow whatever we've got. When the business model that we have doesn't allow us to grow, the job we have can't pay us more money, or the market we are in doesn't allow for much growth, Dynamos end up overextending and going back to Infrared. It's like uprooting a plant you want to grow too soon: The whole plant dies. As the ancient Chinese philosopher Lao-tzu said, "Nature does not hurry, yet everything is accomplished." Don't try to make something grow faster than it should.

Pinpointing our passion then is not about chasing things on the outside and exhausting ourselves and those around us. It is about looking inside to think about what we love most—what would make us jump out of bed every morning—and then connecting that passion to other people who were already in flow and love the same things that we do.

For me, I love creating and adding value to others, so I made a list of companies that shared the same passion. Some of these were companies in publishing that had a passion for property, but many of them were in education as well. If I could connect with some of these companies that were making more money than me and learn from them, I could find ways for me to tap their flow and make more money for all of us in new and different ways that I wasn't even aware of yet. That led to my needing to take the second step.

Step Two: Set Your Standards

- *Do not* rush everything to try to complete an overwhelming to-do list, always filled with more things you want to do than you can manage.
- *Do* identify the people in flow aligned to your passions; compare the standards they have set in managing their focus, time, thoughts, actions, and connections; and then upgrade your own standards to match theirs.

Red Level is where Dynamo Geniuses need to get clear and focused on a plan that prioritizes better connections and small wins based on higher standards. Setting your standards is about your behavior with the people around you. This is not about trying to impose your ideas on them. This about taking the time to learn both what is of true value to them that you can deliver with your genius, and how to deliver that according to *their* standards.

To grow my cash flow, I needed to find people with shared passions and standards at a higher level than me and raise my standards to meet them. Ask yourself the same questions I did to find them: Who out there is already earning at the level I want to be at? Who are the people I could connect with on this level? Where could I meet them?

I started going to networking events within the industry, which I hadn't been doing when I was just trying to make my money from my publishing business. As I became more interested in education, I met a successful entrepreneur, Richard Tan, who ran a company in Singapore called Success Resources. He brought well-known speakers to Singapore from the United States—including John C. Maxwell, Norman Schwarzkopf, and Bill Clinton—and was attracting thousands to his conferences. I was interested in his event business, which didn't have all the expensive printing costs I endured but still was able to reach many people. That led me to step three.

Step Three: Follow the Flow

- *Do not* try to create more of your own flow by pushing your job or business beyond its ability to make you money and digging a hole in a desert.
- *Do* focus on how you can help others increase their flow with you sharing in the benefit you bring, using your Dynamo Genius to link their flow to yours.

When Dynamo Geniuses reach a limit in their flow, we often try to start new businesses all over again. We assume we know what the people we connect with will want and why they will love our ideas, so we spend our time creating something new and then launching it. This approach leaves us in an endless cycle of starting over.

But this third step is finding the flow, not finding your flow. It's still not time to do it all on your own; you must earn that right by climbing farther up the lighthouse. This is the time to earn while you learn.

I learned Richard was bringing in Tom Hopkins, a well-known speaker on property. I approached him and asked him whether he would like to work together on a property seminar while Tom was in town, to which I could bring along all of the subscribers to our magazine. He liked the idea, and we created an event partnership. I knew how to approach my subscribers, but I didn't know how to run an event. Now that I was working with Richard, I got to learn from the inside how to do it. It was hard work, but we managed to attract several thousand people to the event. We had shared the risk and reaped the reward.

In the end, that single deal made me more profit in one *day* than my entire publishing company made in one *year*. Using my natural Dynamo Genius to create and staying focused on climbing the ladder beyond, I learned an entirely new model to achieve my next step to a million (jumping from $800 to $1,600 in monthly personal net cash flow), helped Richard make money, and gave everyone more value.

The Tempo Genius Path Out of Red

When I met Grace Lai, she was in her early twenties and living in Australia. She had just graduated from medical school and had a job that put her at Red Level, but she was uninspired by the idea of just being another medical practitioner. When Grace found out she was a Tempo Genius, she took that to mean she should get involved in trading. After all, Tempos are very good at trading. So she started connecting with some of the people she knew who were trying to trade the stock market.

The problem was, Grace didn't know if any of those people

were making any money. It turned out they were all beginners and had not yet achieved success. Grace asked me what the best way to do it was, and I told her not to do it at all: If you can't answer the question, *Do other people trust me to invest their money?* with a yes, then why are you investing your own?

I told Grace that learning the flow of trading takes time, so she'd better choose an area she was passionate about. Tempo Geniuses like the idea of setting standards and following the flow. The trouble is pinpointing their passion. For Grace, the question was also: How do you move out of Red Level if you are in a job instead of running a business—and how does a Tempo Genius (the opposite of Dynamo) do it differently? Here is what Grace did.

Step One: Pinpoint Your Passion

- *Do not* pick a path based on someone telling you it's a better or faster way to make money. Don't follow a path only for the money.
- *Do* seek people out through your network and research who you would be passionate about working with—passionate enough that even if you didn't achieve all your financial goals, you would find the work fulfilling and energizing.

For Tempos like Grace, moving up from Red Level is not about finding the vehicle to drive you there; it is about knowing what vehicle you want to drive when you find it. Tempos have to look around them to find out what they are passionate about, and for Grace the answer was where she was working: She was passionate about the whole medical field. She was even more excited about the amazing companies in biomedical research, biotechnology, and personalized medicine that were innovating in exciting new ways.

At this point, Grace wrote her Future Vision, which had her running an investment fund for some of the most cutting-edge medical technology to bring an end to certain diseases around the planet. She was making a big difference in the world as well as making a profit for herself and her investors and all those who were taking a risk for the future of medicine.

Grace loved her Future Vision, but the problem was that she had also been offered a scholarship, and Tempos can really get lost in debating options like these. So I asked her to think of herself twenty years down the line: "If you're actually following your path, will it make any difference whether you took the scholarship or not?" She realized that it would not. "Will you be surrounding yourself with the people you'll be working with when you achieve your success?" She answered, "No." So I asked her, "Where do you think you should instead?" The answer was the investment fund.

She began a Twitter account and blog to track the news and people at the cutting edge of future medicine. The answer was now clear: She needed to get out in front of all the people and companies she wanted to be involved with, which led to her step two.

Step Two: Set Your Standards

- *Do not* bury yourself in researching everything, gathering every bit of information and second and third opinions, before taking any action.
- *Do* use your Tempo Genius to combine your research and connections and connect with those in flow within your chosen field, matching their standards of where they are, what they are doing, and what they value.

Setting standards for a Tempo goes beyond doing research in isolation. When Grace started looking for the right people, she found groups around the world, such as Future Med in Silicon Valley and conferences in Europe, where people on the cutting edge of medical technology meet regularly. Grace needed to buy some time to get to those places, so she applied to work as a surgical assistant to a few more surgeons in Australia with that plan in mind. In her application letters, she spelled out her vision of being a part of the whole transformation happening in medicine right now, offered her impeccable credentials, and asked for the surgeons' support: She would work with them if they had the flexibility to allow her to pursue this dream.

Grace got accepted by three of the top surgeons in Australia and developed a part-time structure with all three in which she would be working for months and then take extended time off. In 2013, she managed to take a whole month off to go to conferences in Europe and the United States to meet with people at the highest levels in the industry. With this path she was in her flow, earning more from her contract work, energized, and excited each day. That is where step three comes in.

Step Three: Follow the Flow

- *Do not* try to work it all out on your own or simply take whatever opportunities appear in front of you.
- *Do* use your sensory acuity to see where you can add value profitably to the people you want to work with, following the flow.

Tempo Geniuses turn plans into action. That's why people love having Tempos on their teams. The problems happen when Tempos get stuck having to deliver something they don't know how to or have the time to deliver. Instead, Tempos need to join or create a team where they can earn by helping others earn. Tempos will always be the ones to find smarter ways to manage costs, set the rhythms, and keep things organized. If they stay focused on these strengths, they free up their team's time to dig new tributaries off existing rivers.

That's exactly what Grace did as soon as the money started

flowing to her: She found people interested in her research and social media skills. She formulated services tailored to their needs. She connected to a team that supported her at the standards she set. More important, she bought herself time to go out and connect with people she needed and wanted to connect with to keep following the flow. And she loves every moment of it. What was once a dream is now a reality, all because Tempo Grace is now moving through the flow of other people rather than in isolation.

The Blaze Genius Path Out of Red

While Dynamos need to *grow* and Tempos need to *slow*, Blazes need to *glow*. That is their strength—provided they focus it at the next level. That's what Lucio Fan, who runs an Italian restaurant in Taipei, learned to do to move out of Red.

When I began mentoring Lucio, he wanted to franchise his restaurant across Taiwan. Franchising is a common way to multiply one profitable outlet into many. The problem was, his first restaurant wasn't making money yet. He needed to focus on adding more value to his first outlet *before* he tried to franchise it. "But it isn't so much fun to do that," Lucio told me.

Lucio was also in business with a number of partners and had agreed to a role he really didn't enjoy: managing the financials and performance. Blazes aren't suited to focusing on the books, and Lucio was using every excuse he could to avoid the detailed work, creating chaos for the business and frustration for himself.

The first step was to get Lucio into his passion.

Step One: Pinpoint Your Passion

- *Do not* get distracted by *what* is out there, chasing the many opportunities people present to you and getting busier delivering what they want instead of lighting your inner spark.

- *Do* use your freedom of movement to focus on the *who*— connect your passion to the people you want to work with and then use your Blaze Genius to add value to their flow.

Passion is not a problem for Blazes at any level; focusing on the right passion is. I asked Lucio how he would feel if he was at the restaurant, entertaining guests and potential partners for the future and supporting the growth of the business through the connections he made. He said, "I would love to do that—that's what I really enjoy."

When Lucio wrote his Future Vision, we focused on this passion to enhance the flow of others. We found that Lucio's passion was to entertain. He wanted to host big groups and share his knowledge of Italian history and culture. So we created a vision of an Italian restaurant that was always full, serving the Italian community, enjoying 20 percent profit, attracting investors and franchisees, and with Lucio spending several nights a week entertaining groups there. Now Lucio needed to set higher standards for how he managed his time to realize this vision, and the people he would connect with to realize those standards.

Step Two: Set Your Standards

- *Do not* spread yourself too thin, failing to raise your standards and focus your time and ending up with too many loose ends to tend to.
- *Do* use your Blaze Genius to invest time connecting to those who share your passion and understanding the standards by which they connect and judge success so that you (and your team) can deliver value to them in a way that links their flow to yours.

When we worked out how many groups and themed evenings Lucio would need to reach his profit number, it was just eight in a month. To make this process enjoyable for a Blaze Genius, we turned his numbers into people: "How does the extra profit you need translate into extra seats filled each week?" Then we focused on the actual people: "Who would you want in the seats?" Lucio went to the Italian consulate and invited their members and friends to his themed nights. He went to the tutors who were teaching Chinese people how to speak Italian and gave them special deals to visit.

These were just simple things that Blaze Geniuses like Lucio can do. They love speaking to people and calling people up. Now he had a focused way to do it. Focus comes not just in what you do, but also what you don't do. Blaze Geniuses are constantly distracted and need to learn a simple word: *no*. Lucio stopped doing the finances and brought an accountant in to help.

Step Three: Follow the Flow

- *Do not* pay the most attention to and work with the people who are shouting the loudest and support them by catering to *their* needs.
- *Do* pay attention to the people who can help you achieve *your* goals by supporting what you are doing, sharing your goals, and enhancing their flow.

Blaze Geniuses often have the problem of helping everyone without getting anything in return. That's because Blazes love to be loved and find it difficult to ignore anyone. In Lucio's case, he had people coming in frequently asking for specific discounts. Instead of offering a set menu, he tried to tailor menus for each group. Now, to create a mutually beneficial arrangement, he created specific group packages that limited the choices but still offered the best of the restaurant. For people looking for special prices, he had a lower-priced Sunday brunch that immediately filled up weeks in advance.

As a result, Lucio succeeded by fitting people into his program rather than constantly trying to work around them. At this point, the restaurant excited Lucio every day. Without constantly being distracted, he was able to move from Red Level to a strong Orange with positive cash flow and looking forward to his activities ahead. Five months after we put the plan in place, Lucio hosted an evening for me and twelve friends at his restaurant and shared with me that he had hit all his targets. I congratulated him on the results and told him he was ready to franchise. He turned to me and whispered, "Thank you for that. We have already had people approach us wanting to franchise. But I will only grow if I can keep enjoying evenings like these!"

The Steel Genius Path Out of Red

While Blaze needs to *glow*, Steel needs to *know*. Tapping into the flow is quite different for Steel Geniuses, because they are not out networking naturally every day the way Blaze Geniuses are. Janet Johnson is a Steel Genius who has spent her life as an accountant. When I met her, she had spent many years surviving at Red Level with her UK accounting company, and she was exhausted. She had started in a government job, and when her department was downsized, she had used her accounting skills to take on contracting; she had a small team. Life was not bad, but she felt trapped by what she felt was her only skill set. "This is all I know how to do," she told me.

Janet wanted to get more out of the business but didn't know how, as she was already working long days. She also wanted to get involved with something that could make her more money to provide for her family. Her children were getting older now, and her bills were growing with them.

I told her to stop overanalyzing business models and tap into her Steel Genius. Steel Geniuses are much better off making money by finding time and cost savings for someone else in flow. "Believe me," I said, "your genius is greatly valued by those who have more flow than they can manage." But before a Steel Genius like Janet Johnson could know who those people were, she needed to pinpoint her passion beyond a spreadsheet. Steels can get lost in the numbers they love.

Step One: Pinpoint Your Passion

- *Do not* overanalyze everything looking for answers and relying on research and metrics alone to work out what to do.
- *Do* make a list of the people and companies that are in flow and are having success in an area you could see yourself also being passionate about.

When I asked Janet what she loved most about her job, she answered, "I really like making sure we get our clients' books in order. I love it when I see them use my advice to save money and increase their profits." I asked her which of her clients she liked the most. "The schools," she said.

Turns out, within her school district, Janet's company was the number one provider to the schools—more than 60 percent used her services. That was because she'd started her accounting company when her government job providing those services to the schools was disbanded; those schools then had to start getting their accounts audited privately. Out of a job, she went to the schools she'd been working with and asked if they wanted her to keep handling their accounts. All said yes. The business had grown from there, but she still ended up at zero most months.

That's because she wasn't looking beyond the numbers. If she was passionate about making a difference to the schools, she could raise her standards and look to make an even bigger difference.

Step Two: Set Your Standards

- *Do not* procrastinate and put off decisions, aiming for a different result with the same pattern of behavior that got you here in the first place.

- *Do* use your Steel Genius and freedom of movement to connect with the people you are most passionate about serving, and to learn how you can meet their standards, delivering value beyond their expectation.

Ironically, Steel Geniuses will often find traction by *lowering* their standards instead of *raising* them, as their genius naturally lifts their standards to a level that makes it almost impossible to get started setting new ones. And Janet needed new standards. Clients would only pay so much for the audit that her company did. She needed to ask what other services she could provide. She had the schools' accounting business, but there had to be other ways that she could be generating income from those schools in ways those schools needed.

Identifying what kind of services she thought schools might want was the first step toward raising her standards to meet them. Could she imagine herself just doing business for schools? She could, and she started to reorganize her entire business around schools rather than accounting. She made a list of the schools she had the best relationships with and physically went to meet them to see where they needed more help. Did they need training in cost control? Advice on purchasing IT equipment? Help with their teacher payroll? These questions led to step three.

Step Three: Follow the Flow

- *Do not* try to increase your cash flow by simply doing what you're already doing better or more efficiently.
- *Do* use your analytic skills to learn how you can take your Steel Genius and apply it to areas of greater flow and higher value for the people in flow who trust your ability to deliver.

With a list of possible areas to focus on, Janet started doing surveys of all the schools in her region. She gave them options for how she could support and help. It turned out that the schools really wanted help in areas way beyond accounting. They wanted help buying new equipment. They wanted help managing their payroll and their teams more effectively. They wanted help with choosing the right technology. There were many areas, and yet they didn't need a high-level expert for each area; they just wanted someone they could trust to give them good advice.

Janet realized that after serving as their accountant for so many years, they completely trusted her. She changed the name of her company to Educational Finance Solutions and began by offering training to schools on preparing their accounts for audit. To be more efficient and effective with her own time, she offered webinars teaching ways for schools to save money and then offered her help to realize those solutions.

Today Janet's company offers services including budget planning, completion of school funding applications, recruitment consultancy, and training of new and existing school staff. She now creates a higher cash flow and profit from her training than her accounting, and she has a bigger team of staff and experts to help her. Her profits are multiple times what they had been for the last ten years. She achieved this by realizing how she could deliver more value and ways of doing business by simply following the flow. Janet is now at Yellow Level, on her way to Green.

Clark Kent Time Versus Superman Time

Too often, when we are at Red Level, we read books or watch reality TV shows that tell us we need to persevere on our own to succeed and risk it all to get ahead. Yet the worst thing you can do if you are in a job that you feel trapped by *is to quit*.

Sure, that job may not pay well, you may not enjoy it, and it may feel exciting to jump into the unknown. But the moment you quit your job because a book or expert tells you to—without any cash flow to replace your salary—you go immediately into Infrared. Even if you are tapping into savings you expected to use, you've made a mistake most of us realize too late.

I don't want you to escape work or quit your job. I want you to find and follow the work you love in a way that works best for your genius and where you are today.

You might still be surprised to hear me say this. You might think because of my path that I consider being an entrepreneur and running a business as better than having a job. You may be convinced I agree with the books that say running a business is of higher value on the "wealth ladder" than having a job. I don't. Saying that having a business is better than having a job is like saying having a bus is better than having a car. Whether it is or not depends on the purpose of your pursuit and where you want to go.

Sometimes the best thing we can do is work for others, provided the people we are working for are aligned with our natural path in life and our work helps us climb the steps out of Red. Because here's the truth you just learned from all these stories: *Everybody*—including millionaires and billionaires—works for somebody else. The difference is that if you are on your natural path, work doesn't feel like work.

Too many people at Red Level jump into their own business wanting to be Superman and giving up their Clark Kent job, as if it needs to be all one or all the other instead of just buying the hours you need to learn and connect with others. The most successful wealth creators in the world understand that even Superman needs to be Clark Kent some of the time.

Warren Buffett, one of the richest men in the world and a Tempo Genius, began his investment career working for the value investor Benjamin Graham. He didn't just invest his own money on the stock market and hope for the best. When he learned enough and had built trust and a track record—as Grace Lai is doing—he attracted the funding and support to succeed on his own.

Remember, Superman doesn't get paid to save the world. He needs that Clark Kent newspaper reporter's job some of the time to pay for his stretchy suit and cape. At Red Level, you need to ask, *What is the minimum time I need to spend in Clark Kent Time each week, buying me the rest in Superman Time to pursue my Future Vision?*

When I was at Red Level, I found ways to reduce my time running my business to two days a week, giving me three days to connect with new opportunities, leading to my conference business. Grace bought herself time with her surgical work to attend conferences around the world, with one month of Clark Kent Time and one month of Superman (or Wonder Woman) Time. Both Lucio and Janet managed to reduce their Clark Kent Time to just one day a week with the rest pursuing their new paths.

All of us were still *in* our Clark Kent jobs when we did this so we did not fall back into Infrared.

So don't ever let anyone tell you jobs are for losers, especially if your job is suiting your genius's natural strength. And even if you hate it, it's still a better option than quitting and starting a business that is not naturally suited to you simply because you see bigger dollar signs. If you are earning enough to be at Red Level in your job, use your Superman Time to create something that suits your strength and gets you in flow while you have the job. You'll end up with a life that is far more fulfilling than panicking with no job and returning to the stress and anxiety of Infrared.

Once your income from your Superman Time is high enough to replace your Clark Kent Time, you can hire someone to take on some of your Clark Kent Time. Or that becomes the point when you quit your job and go full-time into your own business. In your Future Vision and Flight Path, based on your cash flow targets, you may already be able to see when that point will be. Perhaps it is three months or six months from now. If you have understanding employers, you may also find that by sharing your vision with them, they support it by giving you flexible hours or contract work to free up your time and leave you more motivated and productive in the times you are working for them.

To do that effectively, you'll need to understand the language of flow.

Learn the Language of Flow: The Difference Between Requests and Opportunities

Remember what I said before: The third step of Red Level is to "Follow *the* Flow," not "Follow *your* Flow."

If you go to a river and dig a new outlet, you end up creating new flow off that river. In fact, after the water begins flowing, it creates its own river down your channel without your needing to dig anymore. The problem is, too many people see this action of *digging* as what they need to do to create flow. But it isn't the action that matters: It's *where* you dig. If you start digging in a desert, you don't dig a river; you dig a hole.

Starting a business without first understanding and then going where there is flow is like digging a hole in the desert: Don't do it!

I don't want you to quit your job, and I don't want you just to go and get a second job. The challenge most people have when they try to get a job in the job market is that the job market is *the most difficult place to get a job.* In the job market, you are in competition with everyone else looking for a job, and you only see the jobs that someone else has already worked out they need.

The people in all the Red Level stories chose or created jobs with the people they wanted to work with. They didn't join the job market. To create wealth, you don't want to be *searching* for a job; you want to be *creating* a job: Wealth creation is about job creation—starting with your own! It isn't money that makes money; it's people who make money. So, it will be other people who will help you make your money.

To do this, you need to use a different language: the *language of wealth*. **The language of wealth is opportunity—the opposite of the language we learned in school.**

When I went to Richard Tan, I did not say, "I need a job" or "I need more money." I asked him, "Would it help you if I could bring more people to see Tom Hopkins?" This is the difference between speaking in requests (*here's what I need*) and speaking in opportunities (*here's what I can offer*).

The language we learned in school is the language of request. If we needed to go to the toilet, we raised our hand and asked to go. If we didn't understand an answer, we asked the teachers to please explain it. Later in life, if we don't have money, we go to the bank and request a loan. In the same way, if we need a job, we say, "Can I have a job?"

These are all requests; we are asking for something that we don't have and need. As a result, the people we are making the requests to are the drivers of our future, not us. Requests are based on what we don't have, and every time you make a request, you are reminding yourself (and others) of what you don't have and giving away your power to make the change.

People at a high level of wealth creation realize that their power comes from making their biggest needs somebody else's biggest opportunity. *Every* need you have is someone else's opportunity. You can go to someone with money and say, "I need money," or you can say, "I have an opportunity for you to get a high return on your investment. Are you interested?" Instead of saying, "I need a job," you can say what Janet did: "What are the biggest problems you are facing that I can help solve?"

Rest assured: Every person and company has challenges they are looking to overcome, and they are looking for solution providers (not problem creators) to help them. Are they looking to sell more products? Become more efficient? Provide better service? Do they want to generate more sales? Make more profit?

For every person who has time but not money, there is someone out there who has money but no time. Time is your greatest asset, and you have the same twenty-four hours as everyone else. Be aware of that and invest it well by focusing on the needs of the people you want to work with instead of your needs. By turning your contribution to fulfill that need into an opportunity for them, you can create a new job that connects your genius to their flow.

When you change all your requests to opportunities, you earn yourself a ticket to the Enterprise Prism. That's because all companies speak in opportunities. They don't tell you, "We need your money for our products and services to pay our rent." They offer opportunities to meet your needs or desires in the form of products and services. They don't say, "We need your help." They offer job opportunities.

There's also a ripple effect of opportunities that requests do not enjoy. When you share your need, it rarely gets passed on. When you share a great opportunity, people share it with the people they know who will benefit from it. People love passing on good news (and good people) to others they know.

When you change from requests to opportunities, you go from a world of lack to a world of abundance. There's a limit to what you can get, but there's no limit to what you can give.

Ready to move up? Now is the time to take advantage of the opportunities your freedom of movement buys and follow the flow. The steps in the following Action Point will help you turn what you need right now into an opportunity for the people you want to work with: to *create* a job, not *find* one.

CHAPTER FOUR SUMMARY

- Red Level has just enough money to have nothing.
- Understand the Ten Steps to a Million: When you put $100 in net cash flow aside each month, you only need to double it ten times before you reach $1 million in extra cash flow every year. This is the ladder up the lighthouse.
- There are three steps to move from Red Survivor to Orange Worker that connect your passion and talents to the flow of the markets. Each genius has a different path and winning formula and losing formula through them:

  Pinpoint Your Passion
  Set Your Standards
  Follow the Flow

- Split your time between Clark Kent and Superman Time: Distinguish what you are doing to earn the money to buy your time and move to Orange Level from what you are doing to connect to the market and to your future flow.
- Learn the language of flow and create opportunities: Your need is someone else's opportunity. When you turn your need into an opportunity, you can create a job instead of needing to find one.

Preflight Checklist: Orange Level

Your personal page on www.millionairemasterplan.com has supplemental guides and videos, including assessments and Playbooks, for each of the checklist points below. I have included one of the exercises from the Playbook at the end of this chapter: Creating your own job through the Five Steps to Follow the Flow.

These steps to move out of Red Level are for surviving *and* ensuring you are constantly upgrading your own personal flow and standards. Too often we reach a plateau in our wealth creation and contribution. These steps will ensure you don't! Complete the checklist now: Tick yes or no. How do you rate? When all nine are checked yes, you will have connected your personal passion and purpose to your Flight Path.

Pinpoint Your Passion

1. I have a Passion Board of activities, people, and things that electrifies and inspires my Flight Path and daily life. ☐ Yes ☐ No

2. I have a list of the companies and people I connect with who are in flow and share the same passions as me. ☐ Yes ☐ No

3. I ensure that I have designed my rhythm and chosen the people I work with to keep me aligned in my passion and purpose. ☐ Yes ☐ No

Set Your Standards

1. I have a Standards Sheet of the new higher standards I have set and the old standards I will no longer settle for. ☐ Yes ☐ No

2. I seek out and surround myself with people who are living at the same standards that I have chosen for myself. ☐ Yes ☐ No

3. I ensure I have designed my life to suit my profile and strengths so that I stay in my flow. ☐ Yes ☐ No

Follow the Flow

1. I have connected with companies and people in flow that I am earning positive cash flow from, earning as I learn. ☐ Yes ☐ No

2. I am investing my time in connecting with the people and opportunities in my chosen industry to grow my flow. ☐ Yes ☐ No

3. I am measuring the growth in my knowledge and network and have clear pathways to deliver my value. ☐ Yes ☐ No

ACTION POINT

Five Steps to Follow the Flow

I f you have been in a job all your life or had little experience understanding what people need and how you can use your genius to serve them profitably, you may be used to just following instructions without needing to identify someone's problem and help solve it. That's how you end up trapped in a job or unemployed waiting for someone to throw you a lifeline.

All successful business owners or investors could start all over again if their business failed, because they have built the ability to find out what people need and then deliver against that. They know this skill set is the best form of job security anyone can have today.

Everyone you read about in this book asked these five questions and used the answers to connect with those already in flow.

Question 1—What are the criteria for the job you are going to create?

You have set your Future Vision and your Flight Path, so you know how much extra money you want to be making to move you to Orange Level. Set the amount of Superman Time you can put toward this goal each week. Set the specific amount of money you want to achieve in that time.

Now look at your genius and the current skill sets and experience you have: Write a list of the criteria you would want the job you create to meet, where you can feel confident you can add value to the people you will be approaching. What are the activities you would be energized by and confident in doing? Here are some ideas to get you started:

- **Dynamo Geniuses** are natural at adding revenue to a business by introducing a new product or service that existing customers want, being a marketing partner, bringing in new customers for existing products, taking on some planning or strategy activities to free up top revenue producers to produce even more, or running a new promotion with a creative marketing campaign to get happy customers to refer their networks.

- **Blaze Geniuses** are natural at adding revenue to a business by being a marketing partner or an affiliate and going out to their network with existing products, sharing the message and meeting new customers at events or conferences, getting on the phone and speaking to existing customers to find out what they need and want to buy, and creating partnerships with others who can add value through their network or products.

- **Tempo Geniuses** are natural at adding profit to a business by organizing the top producers to be more productive, finding savings in how the business is spending, experimenting with pricing to see what customers are really willing to pay, and helping to deliver a better level of service to existing customers so there are fewer cancellations or more follow-up purchases and referrals.

- **Steel Geniuses** are natural at adding profit to a business by analyzing the numbers and finding ways to save costs, changing systems to improve cash collections, automating costly activities to make them more efficient and cost efficient, providing analysis and data to the top producers so they can direct themselves toward highest-value activities and clients, and creating systems for online sales, renewals, service, and communications.

Question 2—Who would you be most passionate working with on this path?

What people will you have gotten to know in your Future Vision? What is the industry you are most passionate about or the market you would most love to serve? Who are the leaders in the industry that you would love to have a chance to work with and learn from? Make a list of at least ten people and companies. Research. Ask around. Each person you talk to will know of others who you may not know about. Don't assume you already know it all; go out with a fresh curiosity.

Remember: You are not just looking for the best. You are looking for the ones you have a trusted connection with. Either because they know you or because they know someone you know. Make sure each person or company you list is in flow and making money with an opportunity to make more. Once you have your list, narrow it down to the top three and focus on them. Be prepared to replace the ones that begin to feel like dead ends, but be confident that creating your job will happen with one of them. It isn't a matter of *whether* it happens. It is just a matter of *when*.

Question 3—What is the need they have that you can fulfill?

Have a look at what opportunities each of your top three is already offering. They may already have partnership opportunities or be working well with others. Find out what their biggest problems and opportunities are. Find out what they need and how it links with the criteria you set.

If you are already connected with decision makers—people accountable for growing revenue or profit, not necessarily the founders or CEOs—then great. Meet with these people and tell them you love what they do and are committed to being of value to support them and willing to prove yourself. What would they love to see different in a perfect world? What are their biggest challenges? Where do they see themselves a year from now?

Don't try to offer solutions to these challenges yet; just listen. Then connect with others in the company—with partners, with the decision maker's gatekeeper (usually an assistant or project leader)—and write a list of at least three things that you believe you can help them with. Work out what that would mean to them in extra revenue or profit.

Question 4—How can you deliver value with your genius to grow their flow?

You have now identified how you can be of true value to impact a business. This does not happen overnight, but if you work on this with the support of your team, you will find it does not take many weeks to get to this point. The time has come to put your plan into action and put a trial in place.

From the responses you receive, you will narrow down your decision to work with one company and focus all your efforts on them for your trial. Be prepared to work for nothing first to prove yourself, knowing you are getting to choose your own job if you can do so.

A month trial is a good start and use of your Superman Time. What could you achieve in a one-month trial? How much revenue or profit will you aim to help them make? What other metrics would you include: Time freed for the decision maker? Putting a new system in place?

The first step is to make people know you are committed to serving them. The second step is to propose your project to them. Be upfront that you want to prove yourself first before asking for anything in return, but that you are also committed to making the extra cash flow you want. Based on your success, what level of results would you need to achieve to earn what you need to earn? Through your helping them, they will help you achieve that.

More often than not, people who commit to this process not only end up working with someone on their Top 10 list within a matter of months, if not weeks, but often the company decides to find a role and pay them.

Question 5—How will they and you profit from your partnership?

Every company is willing to pay something to a partner or contractor who is able to bring them new business or improve their revenues or profits. Exactly how much will depend on the type of business. Online businesses with electronic products will give as much as 70 percent of their revenues away to affiliates that can help them grow their revenue. Service businesses will give up to 50 percent away; product businesses will give away 5 to 20 percent; and asset-based businesses like property will give far less, because the asset cost is so much greater.

Through conversations and research, find out how money in the company is normally split when it forms a partnership or brings in help. Agree on the basics: What are you going to do? What is the benefit to them? What happens if you are successful? (Do you get paid and a longer-term partnership or role begins?)

What are you waiting for, Superman? Keep yourself positive with your Clark Kent Time and answer these five questions to create the job that gets you on the inside.

FROM ORANGE TO YELLOW: WORKER TO PLAYER

Measure:	Positive personal cash flow controlled by others
Emotions:	Dependence; resignation
Cost of staying here:	Anonymity; fear; frustration
Focus needed:	Identity and independence
How did I get here?	Education; mind-set; conditioning
How do I move up?	Identify Your Identity; Master Your Market; Monetize Your Moment

Welcome to Orange Level. The air is much clearer up here: you can see there is more than just "getting by" at Red Level. You are in positive cash flow. You feel some sense of direction. Even if you are in a well-paying job you don't love, at least you are moving forward and in a better position to move up than those who quit and slipped back down to Red or Infrared. You have a deeper sense of self-worth, especially as others often acknowledge the good work you do.

But you are still dependent on those "others" to get by. Maybe you have a job and haven't yet found your own identity in the market. Perhaps you have a business, but you haven't been able to create an identity that attracts others, so you still need to chase the money. You might have overextended yourself with properties or assets that went negative, leaving you dependent on working in a job or in your business to get by. Or you may have just climbed here from Red Level (congratulations if so!) and now want to figure out how to master your market, multiply your income, and attract the flow of wealth to you.

Regardless of your circumstance, you work hard for a living at Orange Level. On the one hand, extra cash does come in constantly so you don't have that same level of anxiety as Red Level; on the other hand, you are constantly chasing business, and the end of the week comes as a relief.

Being an Orange Worker used to be enough to live a good life. Our grandparents' or parents' generations could work hard, stay at one company most of their working days, and have the money to retire when they stopped. Today the world is far less secure. True security only comes from designing your own pathway and moving from dependence at Orange Level to independence at Yellow Level, where you have your own boat and sail it wherever you choose instead of being a passenger on a boat that could sink at any time.

Yellow Level is a very different feeling than Orange Level because you earn money from your opportunities, partnerships, products, and services instead of by trading your time. You are no longer chasing the flow; you are focused on a niche and people (customers, partners, and staff). The business shows up for you. Opportunities get attracted to you because of your position in the market. You make money far more easily and have a real sense of participation in the markets.

How do you do that? Before you follow your genius's path through the three steps out of Orange, let me let you in on a secret that you can understand by reaching Orange Level: All flow in every system is made up of just two things. **Everything from your personal finances to the finances of very big companies to entire economies is made up of** *projects* **and** *processes.*

Projects and Processes

Projects are things that add flow, like new roads. Dynamo and Blaze Geniuses love projects and adding new products and relationships to the flow. The problem is that many of us try to start new projects— creating extra income, getting a new job, or starting a business— and find they cost time and money that we don't have. Or we start a project that creates a traffic jam or creates a road that goes nowhere. I've seen people write books or put up websites that end up taking a lot of time but doing nothing to help them create any flow or make any money when the project is complete.

Processes are things that maintain flow, like a road that links to other roads. Any block or break leads to a problem on a road, like a traffic jam. Similarly, any block or break in our financial flow leads to a financial problem. Tempo and Steel Geniuses love processes for restoring, maintaining, and improving this flow. The problem is that most of us are stuck in the middle of our processes, directing the traffic instead of outsourcing or automating the flow so we can get off the road and back to enhancing and expanding our system.

In the Foundation Prism, we are all participating in other people's projects and processes; it is our money or time going into their plumbing system as consumers or workers.

In the Enterprise Prism, we get rewarded for adding to or maintaining the global plumbing system as creators and employers.

To move to Yellow Level and the Enterprise Prism, you need to look at what processes you are spending time on and see what you can outsource or automate. Then the trick is to turn your projects into profitable projects.

I call these profitable projects promotions. Other wealth creators might call them campaigns, but the terms mean the same thing: projects that create new flow, enable new learning, and make money. Based on past experience and best guesses, you set a path, a beginning and an end, and milestones along the way so you know what value you want to deliver and when you want to deliver it. Based on your level, it may be a promotion to create $100, $1,000, or more in new cash flow. You then use this to get the job you want, start the right business, make the right investment, create a new partnership, and more. You don't need to have all the answers to the *Who?* and *How?* yet. You just need to answer the questions, *What are my goals?* and *What are the milestones I want to reach and when will I reach them?* (The Action Point at the end of this chapter helps you come up with your own promotion, and your personal page on www.millionairemasterplan.com has links to a detailed Promotions Playbook to move you forward even farther.)

Once you become aware of the anatomy of a promotion, you will see that wealth creators in any industry—retail, publishing, travel, speaking, training, tech start-ups, online marketing, network marketing, property, financial markets, financial services, and so on—follow the most effective promotion models for their industries to earn and learn. They test and measure against their assumptions and then often share best practices with each other. The unsuccessful leaders simply open up shop, get busy, chase the business, and hope for the best.

Understanding how to use your genius to create a promotion allows you to raise your monthly cash flow far higher than time alone allows. My first publication, my first event, my first property purchase and sale, my first business launch and sale... each of these was a promotion that allowed me to make the money I wanted, attract the resources and partnerships I needed, and test and measure the results.

Most important, as we get better at predicting and replicating the results of our promotions, we attract the higher-quality partners we need to climb from Yellow Player to Green Performer to Blue Conductor. Making sure you understand how the Power of Zero and the Wealth Equation relate to your promotions and to the Ten Steps to a Million we covered in the last chapter is essential before starting this climb.

The Power of Zero

How did I and how will you take the Ten Steps to a Million—from $1,600 net cash flow each month to $3,200, $6,400, and beyond? Through the *Power of Zero*. Think about what feels like a lot to you now. When I was twenty-two and my mentor challenged me to make an extra $100 each month, I thought that was easy. When he said I could make an extra $100,000 each month, I thought he was crazy. So what feels like a lot of money to you in terms of those zeroes? Is it $10, $100, $1,000, $10,000, or more?

What is the amount of money you would really notice if it disappeared from your bank account tomorrow?

When I was seven, I received pocket money of 50 cents each week. I thought, *If I save up my pocket money, I can buy a bicycle like my friend Paul got for his birthday.* I didn't take the time to work out how many months or years I would need to save. I just remember saving, and after one month I had two dollars. Five months later, I had ten dollars. Then we moved to a new house, and in the move I lost my piggy bank. I literally lost all the money in my piggy bank! It was heartbreaking. Ten dollars was like a million dollars to me then.

More than a decade later, when I was in Cambridge and ran my first little business as a student, I was at Red Level; $10 was no longer a lot to me. But $100 was. So when I got to Red Level, I wouldn't miss $10, but $100 was a real buying decision. From there, each time I climbed a level in the lighthouse, I added a zero onto what I considered a lot of money. By the time I got to Orange,

I wouldn't miss $100 because there was more money flowing, but $1,000 became a risk. By the time I moved through Yellow Level, $10,000 was not so much (I was used to seeing that move rapidly in the day-to-day of the team), but $100,000 was a stretch to risk or lose.

Simply put, I earned the right to play with more zeroes at the next level by achieving the level below naturally and automatically. Adding a zero to what I was willing to comfortably lose (and a zero to what I was able to make) in my promotions unlocked a new code—a new language—which we all need in order to listen with clarity and speak fluently at the level above.

The time it took me to complete a moneymaking project also changed as I moved up the lighthouse. Starting at Red and moving up to Orange Level, I could deliver results within a week of starting a new project. At Yellow Level, the time to complete a new promotion stretched to one to three months (like my publications and events). At Green Level, it was a year. And at Blue Level today, I have promotions that last three to five years, including building and selling businesses, properties, or other assets.

By focusing at the right size and speed of your promotions, as you rise up the levels one step at a time, you can turn what felt like a lot to something that you know is much easier to make. You can also do it *at the right pace*. Too many people shoot for $10,000 promotions when they haven't yet mastered $1,000 promotions; they're out of their depth the moment they begin.

While promotions in the Foundation Prism are largely based around using your time and genius to connect to the flow of others, Yellow Level promotions are larger because you are now engineering new sources of flow—launching a new product, starting a new partnership, or entering a new market. But before we see how each genius does this, there is one final tool you need in your toolbox to master the Enterprise Prism that I learned in my first promotion: the Wealth Equation.

The Wealth Equation:
Wealth = Value × Leverage

I was eighteen years old and finishing my first year at college. My friends were all planning a trip to Greece, and I didn't have the $800 I needed to join them. My director of studies had also just told me that unless I added more work to my architecture portfolio, I was in danger of failing. On top of this, I really wanted to attend the rowing camp that was taking place at end of term. How could I add to my portfolio if I was busy working somewhere? How would I even find the time to earn money in a job if I was also attending the rowing camp?

Then, one evening, the proverbial lightbulb went on above my head: Instead of asking all these questions separately and seeing only conflicting challenges, I combined them into one question: *How do I earn $800 while adding to my portfolio, with enough time left over to attend rowing camp?*

I came up with a plan to answer this question and gave myself one week to make $400 to gauge my progress. That was how much money my friends were making in their summer jobs in London. If I could do that, I wouldn't need to get a job myself.

I went to rowing camp each morning, but for the first three days, I went to a different tourist site in Cambridge immediately afterward: King's College Chapel, Trinity Gate, and St. John's Street. I sketched pictures of each in black and white, had them copied onto good paper, went to the supermarket to buy freezer bags, and put the prints in each bag. On the fourth day, I picked a busy spot where tourists were passing by, and I set myself up with a bag and a sign that said: LIMITED PRINTS OF CAMBRIDGE BY ARCHITECTURE STUDENT. ONE PRINT FOR $6. TWO PRINTS FOR $10. I began drawing a fourth picture while I waited to sell my prints.

It was slow going to begin with; by lunchtime I only had $40. So I began to experiment. I divided my time into fifteen-minute blocks and tracked when I sold prints and when I didn't. It turned out that when a group stopped, everyone stopped and bought, but if no one stopped, I didn't sell anything. So I started looking out for people who weren't so busy and struck up conversation. They stopped, a crowd stopped, and my sales doubled.

By the end of the first day I had worked out that when I asked a child if he or she would like to watch me draw, an entire family would stop, and they would stay for twice as long. Again, my hourly sales doubled. By the end of the first day, I had more than $230. I repeated the process the next day, and at the end of two days of selling, I had five new pictures for my portfolio and over $400 in my pocket—my target for the week!

I was extremely curious to see if the second week would be a repeat of the first. But in the middle of the second week, I plateaued at just over $200 a day. This still meant I made all the money I needed for the Greece trip within a week, and I realized I was earning a lot more than my friends in London. But what excited me more was watching and learning how flow moved just by interacting with people and how it changed over time. I wondered whether there were still ways to double the money I was making for the same effort.

Turns out there were. As with all promotions where you are testing and measuring your results against a target, often the big breaks come by accident. It was about eleven in the morning of the second week, and I had just begun sketching a new picture while sitting on a new street corner. An American tourist and his wife stopped, and we got into a conversation. I asked if he would like to buy some of my prints. He looked at the new drawing I had just started and said, "No, but I would like to buy that."

My original! I laughed, "No, I can't sell this. I'll make prints of this after and sell them, so I need to keep it."

"Everything has a price," he said. "How much?"

I thought about that. I could decide that the value of the original was thousands of dollars if I calculated all the prints I would sell of it, or I could determine that it was just an hour of my time and sell it for that. Then it occurred to me that if I sold it for $200, I could take the rest of the day off.

"It'll cost $200," I said.

"Done," he replied, "But can you sign it as well?"

So I wrote at the bottom "Unfinished Original" and signed my name. He paid me $200 and then walked off with his wife.

I sat in silence, looking at the money. I looked at my watch. It was 11:15 a.m. I had the entire day ahead of me. I could do anything I wanted! What would I do? I looked at my blank sketchpad. I looked at the scene I had just been drawing. I pulled out a blank sheet of paper and began drawing the same scene all over again. By the end of the day, I had my finished picture to start another income stream, another $200 earned plus the $200 from the American tourist, and I had doubled my earnings to $400 a day.

Each day after that, I spent the first hour creating an unfinished original, signing it, posting it for sale, and beginning again. By the time I left for Greece I had earned more than I could imagine. My friends looked at me strangely when I showed up with all that cash in my rucksack.

You could say that my story required many pieces of luck and fortunate timing, not just artistic skill and a little inventiveness. I needed to be in a tourist town. I had to know how to draw pictures interesting enough that people would want to buy them. But in every promotion I have been a part of over the last thirty years, there has always been some luck. When you plan a promotion, you are directing all your actions to specific results and leaving the door open for magic to happen and luck to occur.

This little promotion was where I caught the entrepreneurial bug and sowed the seed for my future. In the end, my real success was not what I started with, but what I learned and adjusted through the process, especially my coming to understand—for the first time—the equation to wealth. It explains how we, like plumbers, can direct flow effectively using our genius, and it is an essential part of moving up to Yellow Level.

Wealth = Value × Leverage

Imagine a river: Water flows where there is a height differential. Similarly, money flows where there is a value differential, based on value exchange. When people bought my prints for $6, it meant they valued my prints equal to or more than the price I set. I end up with their money, and they end up with my prints. Every day, trillions of dollars of money flows naturally in this way.

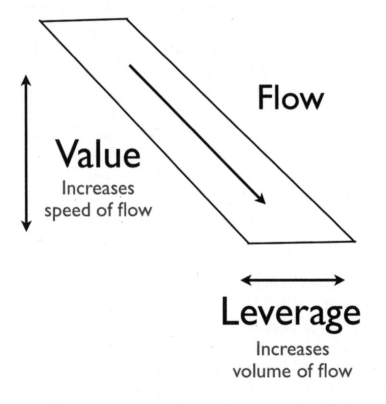

Value controls the speed of money flow. It is the grade of the river. Leverage is the width and controls the volume of money flow. By making copies of my drawings, I was leveraging the value so I could sell the same picture twice or a hundred times with the same effort to draw it but a much bigger potential payoff. Leverage. When the tourist bought my unfinished original, he saw greater value in my hour's work than my leverage was rewarding me for a day's work. But he may not have paid so much if I was not selling so many of my prints. My leverage led to new value.

Between value and leverage all great wealth creators control and grow flow. They create value, and they leverage it. Delivering more value is what it feels like when you accelerate a car by putting your foot on the gas. Leveraging your value is what it feels like when you shift up the gears, and at any moment, you can increase your cash flow by creating new value or adding new leverage.

All the case studies to come involve understanding this equation. They take the first steps to moving from leveraging time to leveraging products or partnerships, which eventually leads to leveraging the expertise of others and entire teams in the Enterprise Prism. That's where you get into property, markets, and businesses, which all have value that you can leverage.

Are you stuck not earning enough right now? There are ways that you can deliver more value, often by changing who you are delivering it to or whose value you are combining with. Are you stuck with not enough time? There are ways that you can leverage your value, letting you earn more with less time, often the same way great wealth creators do: Work together with others to leverage each other's value. Simple? No, not quite.

There are two opposites of value and two opposites of leverage. Too often, we follow a strategy that is the opposite of our own natural genius. Understanding these opposites allows us to see how we can apply our genius to add value and leverage effectively in our markets:

Value is created from our ideas and senses—our thinking

dynamic. Its two opposites are Innovation (Dynamo Genius) and Timing (Tempo Genius):

- Dynamo Geniuses have an "intuitive" thinking dynamic and create value best through innovation. Dynamos see the future and move things forward. At every level of the Wealth Lighthouse, Dynamo Geniuses take the creative route to flow.
- Tempo Geniuses have a "sensory" thinking dynamic and create value through timing. Tempos know when to buy, when to sell, when to act, and when to hold. At every level of the Wealth Lighthouse, Tempo Geniuses take the sensory route to flow.

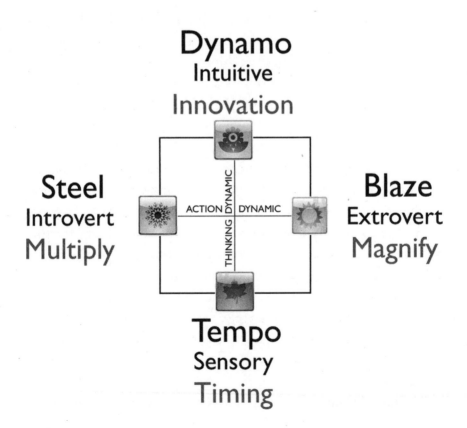

Value is leveraged through our internal and external actions—our action dynamic. The two opposites of leverage are Multiply (Steel Genius) and Magnify (Blaze Genius):

- Steel Geniuses have an "introvert" action dynamic and create leverage through multiplication by asking the question, *How can I do this without me?* Steel Geniuses ascend the Wealth Lighthouse by focusing on the detail and creating systems to build their flow.
- Blaze Geniuses have an "extrovert" action dynamic and create leverage through magnification by asking the question, *How can this only be done with me?* Blaze Geniuses ascend the Wealth Lighthouse by growing their relationships.

When you know how to package, price, promote, and present value in line with your natural genius, you give yourself the power to turn on your own flow. This is the first step in mastering flow: knowing how to control and redirect it by packaging value and exchanging it for new streams of income. This can be through your own products or services, a deal, or a trade. It doesn't take money to make this happen. It takes connection to existing streams of knowledge, opportunity, and flow, and your own commitment to being curious and resourceful while adding value through your unique identity.

The payoff in the Enterprise Prism is that you stop working for money, and money starts working for you.

Three Steps to Move From Orange to Yellow

Do you know what exact actions you can take right now that will put an extra $10,000 in your personal bank account within three months? If you don't, it is because you have not mastered the following three steps to get to Yellow Level. You don't have a close enough connection with your market that you know what value you can offer, how to price that value, and how to approach your market with a promotion compelling enough to attract its players.

At Orange Level, you leave the understanding of how value is leveraged to create cash flow to your employer. You are simply a link in the value chain. To get to Yellow Level, you need to understand the chain and know not just what part you play in that chain but also how you assemble the other parts to ensure you create sustainable cash flow.

Here are the three steps to move from Orange to Yellow:

1. **Identify Your Identity**: To own a place within the global money plumbing system, you first need to choose your specific position: What will you be number one at? What will be your niche? (Read the following paths but also check out the assessments and Playbooks at www.million airemasterplan.com to identify your market identity.)
2. **Master Your Market**: Defining your identity defines your market position, which means you have committed to a market that you must now master. To become a leading player in that market, you must learn who and where its players are, the market size, and the latest developments in that market. What is the profile of your perfect customer? What are their needs and dreams? In today's fast-moving economies, this mastery is paramount.
3. **Monetize Your Moment**: Plan and run promotions that pass your value to your market and put money in your pocket. You need a compelling offer on a particular product or service and a daily focus on whether the results are matching their plan, testing and measuring each day.

Just like the three steps to get out of Infrared and Red, each genius has a different winning and losing formula or path through these steps. Go ahead and read your genius first, but you *must* read the other three after to understand how your winning and losing formula connects and differs from the others.

Every industry, business opportunity, and profession has and needs a mix of geniuses to thrive. You can choose your industry or opportunity based on your passion in Orange Level and then be of value in a way that makes the most of your genius. But when you get to Yellow Level and the Enterprise Prism, you will need a team or partnerships with people already in flow to move you up to Green.

The Steel Genius Path Out of Orange

Hattie Hasan was a plumber in the north of England, stuck in Orange Level. As a female plumber, she got business from women who were alone during the day and didn't want a male plumber in the house. But when I met her, she told me she was working hard chasing the business. Finding new clients was a challenge, and as a perfectionist, she also struggled with the idea of hiring another person to help her.

A Steel Genius, Hattie seemed to sense that her path out of Orange was to multiply, which meant licensing and franchising. To do this, though, she needed a team to make things run more efficiently and get her in flow most rapidly. She needed to partner with a Dynamo Genius to drive things forward creatively and a Blaze Genius to connect to the market. Here are the three steps Hattie took to do that and move from Orange to Yellow and then Green.

Step One: Identify Your Identity

- *Do not* get stuck on the minutiae and metrics, trying to analyze your way to greater efficiency and higher sales.
- *Do* focus on what you uniquely stand for and what you want to be known for, and make it compelling enough that people will pass on the message.

Hattie had been using her Steel Genius to focus on keeping her costs low for the business she had coming in, trying to find smarter and better ways to do the work and still support her clients. But in a cutthroat industry, no matter how much she tried to be efficient and have the best pricing in the industry, someone was always lower.

Steel Geniuses get caught up in details and market data. But that's not what it's about at this point. The question is: *Who do you want to become?* Hattie told me the whole reason that she became a plumber was because she didn't like to have male tradesmen invading her house every time something needed to be fixed. She believed that women plumbers were as good as if not better than men. Why should they not also have an opportunity to work in the trade?

Having a Dynamo Genius like me to talk with allowed her to think about *what she could do* as opposed to *how she could do it*. She thought about what she loved to do and how she could make it her goal as a company to train women to be plumbers and have a job after they did. Hattie then started researching whether there were any other women-only plumbing businesses out there. There weren't, and she decided that was going to be the focus of her business. If she could claim that unique identity, she could base her business around something other than the lowest price in the market, which led her to step two.

Step Two: Master Your Market

- *Do not* overreach by trying to spread yourself thin in too wide a market, being remote and out of touch with the people you are serving.
- *Do* use your Steel Genius to analyze a specific niche and work with Blaze Geniuses to connect with your customers and partners, ensuring you know what they need and what price they are willing to pay for your solutions.

Mastering a market is about understanding what others are doing in that market and what your specific customers really want. Hattie used her Steel Genius to conduct a series of surveys and found out there was a real demand from women for a women-only plumbing business. Through this process she also attracted women who were interested in becoming plumbers—especially if they knew all their clients were also only women. She now knew what she wanted to be known for: the founder of the first all-woman plumbing company in England.

Hattie next decided to set up a business model that connected the two pieces and was perfectly suited to her genius: She could train women plumbers to her perfectionist standards and then set them up with their own plumbing businesses under her brand marketed to women.

Problem was, she needed to revisit step one and give this new business an identity. She struggled initially to find one but then came up with a brand name that immediately had the impact she wanted, a play on a British plumbing device and slang for the male anatomy: Stopcocks.

Step Three: Monetize Your Moment

- *Do not* get caught up in daily activity with no light at the end of the tunnel.
- *Do* focus on using your mastery of process to set up a profitable promotion with clear milestones to create cash flow while developing a system to multiply your value.

Even when they manage to find an identity and the right market, Steel Geniuses at Orange Level often fail to set up their promotion. Whereas a Blaze or Dynamo Genius at this point gets lost chasing opportunities and Tempos get lost in activity, Steel Geniuses revert to their tendency to minimize risk.

Hattie's solution was to set up a promotion that would suit her

Steel Genius and her team with the goal of setting up the systems and processes of her own activity as the model for all her licensees to follow. She assembled the team to support her, attracting great talent inspired by her vision and branding. Her work became easier and more meaningful as she tested and measured everything, envisioning all the woman plumbers and clients who would be benefiting from her work in the future. With the brand and license model in place, attraction and flow continued to grow.

Today, Stopcocks is a national company with woman plumbers all over England. Hattie has never deviated from her niche, though she has expanded the service she offers and now has the business she always wanted—as well as more time than ever to keep making that vision grow.

The Blaze Genius Path Out of Orange

Whereas Steel Geniuses focus on structure and clarity to move up to Yellow Level, Blaze Geniuses are all about the people. When I met Bea Benkova, she was coaching women leaders in London, one of many leadership coaches chasing business in the city and relying mostly on word-of-mouth and referrals. She knew she wanted to work with women, but other than that she was not sure what she stood for and how to design her business to ensure that it took her to where she wanted to go.

So we looked a little farther out: "Imagine yourself five years in the future," I said. "You are being invited on stage to speak to a thousand people about your success. You are introduced with a one-paragraph bio. It includes who you are, what you stand for, and what you have achieved. How would you want your bio to read five years from now? What will be the identity of your future self?"

When Bea answered my question about her future identity, she saw herself as a part of the global movement happening with women in leadership. I told her that her challenge was that who she wanted to be and the services she provided were all rolled into one, which meant that she was confusing her personal brand with her company brand, and she didn't even have a product brand. She needed to set a very clear destination, starting with her identity, and to make sure the people who showed up wanted to go to that destination with her.

Step One: Identify Your Identity

- *Do not* try to be everything to everyone, saying yes to every possibility of business and trying to serve every person you meet.
- *Do* make a clear stand for who you are and who you are not, so when people show up to work with you, they already want to go where you want to take them; and when people refer you to others, it is for a specific niche.

A Blaze Genius trying to be everything to everybody at Orange Level is like a restaurant that serves everything without ever being known for anything. Customers walk in and ask what's good and you say, "What do you want to eat?" You'll make anything for them. Pizza? Sure. Indian food? Of course we can do that. People may come in initially, but it will be difficult for anyone to refer people to you, because no one is sure what your restaurant is about.

Being all things to all people—standing for nothing and falling for everything—is not the way to go. You need to stay focused if you want people to recommend exactly what you are doing. Bea created a clear identity for herself by deciding she would be a voice for woman leadership not in London, where so many competed against each other, but in her native Czech Republic, where she would be able to stand out. She created an organization, the Global

Institute for Extraordinary Women, and a suite of certifications, beginning with the "Femina Fusion" Certification Program.

Step Two: Master Your Market

- *Do not* chase the business around you, getting distracted by the agendas and needs of others with no clear milestones for you (and them) to meet.
- *Do* strategically segment your market by understanding who your customers and partners are and how you can be the number one solution to their needs.

Once Blazes have their identity identified, they want to get out to everybody they can and inevitably fall back into the "being all things to all people" trap. Blazes and their fire energy are always tempted to run around trying to light their bonfire in many different places, which never works as well as focusing on one spot and lighting it there. Instead, you need to build teams to help create, test, and measure the specific products that will serve your customers and partners. While you are out getting feedback, your team can be putting the products and systems together, with you assessing the quality of what is being delivered.

Bea learned that she had three levels of customer in her market: women looking for inspiration and connection to get started in their business or career, successful women who were looking to unite in a meaningful way, and women leaders with their own networks who were looking for partnerships to grow their own missions. Knowing her market helped her decide on her first promotions to launch her institute.

Step Three: Monetize Your Moment

- *Do not* focus on working hard and chasing the next customer without a clear promotion plan that both you and your customers can follow.

- *Do* prioritize your actions in a plan that ensures that every moment of effort is being channeled toward profitable activity that moves you forward.

For all their people skills, Blazes are not strong when it comes to pitching partners, because they are unsure exactly what they want or need. They need to have a clear picture of exactly what they want to achieve and give potential partners and team members a very clear way of seeing how they can work with them to create promotion partnerships. In other words, don't get caught up in trying to answer the question, *What should I do?* Instead, ask yourself, *Who has the right* what*? Who has the wood that I can turn into fire?* Blazes need a Tempo Genius to support them with their timing and a Steel Genius to handle the details. Make sure you agree on the direction and milestones together as a team or you will get unfocused rapidly, skipping from one project to another.

With her new vision, Bea attracted a team of people willing to volunteer time in the early days to support her Global Institute. She set her financial Flight Path and saw that she could generate the money to support herself and the institute with a promotion specifically to a dozen women who would join a twelve-month founders' circle, benefit from mentoring and networking, and be the early success stories for the institute. With this new promotion, all it took was a few days of phone calls to the people who already knew and trusted her, and she had filled her mentoring circle.

By magnifying her value, she got her funding in place, and she set up her second promotion to multiply her value: a book on her story that would shine a light on the institute. Blazes have difficulty promoting themselves but not a cause they believe in. The institute became Bea's cause, and six months later, book in hand, she generated nationwide press with appearances on TV and the national media, which led to more interviews. Three months later, Bea found herself in a panel discussion on national TV with the prime minister.

Bea has continued to grow her Global Institute for Extraordinary Women from one promotion to the next, and now that the fire has been ignited in the Czech Republic, she is taking it around the world. Just twelve months after launch, Bea started forming the international partnerships she was dreaming of, including a thirty-day women's retreat in Bali in partnership with an Australian woman leadership group.

The Tempo Genius Path Out of Orange

Many hopeful wealth creators begin their path of entrepreneurship through a self-employed network, such as being a property or insurance agent, joining a franchise or license network like Hattie's Stopcocks Women Plumbers, or becoming part of a network marketing organization. In all these cases, success does not lie in the network (each can point to successful members earning great income within the network). Success lies in whether you are operating at Orange Level and chasing the business or at Yellow Level and attracting the business to you with a clear personal identity that stands out and makes you the number one choice for your market and clear promotions.

Kevin and Tamsine Harris's network marketing business, Network 21, is one of the largest in South Africa with more than twenty thousand distributors. But they faced a challenge familiar to so many in network marketing: Many of their distributors were chasing the same business.

Kevin and Tamsine were at Yellow Level at this point, but they needed their leaders to take their teams to Yellow, too, if they were going to reach Green Level. That would never happen if those leaders spent all their time chasing the business and competing with each other as opposed to creating their own identities to trade on. At the same time, while some people were naturally attracting business and their networks were growing rapidly, others were pushing and pushing business away. How could the successful Orange-to-Yellow Level thinking be packaged for their entire network?

Kevin is a Blaze Genius and Tamsine is a Tempo Genius. They approached me to see what we could do together to bring the Millionaire Master Plan to their network. The result was Network Dynamics: a promotion we rolled out to their network in Cape Town and Johannesburg with the following three steps and results.

Step One: Identify Your Identity

- *Do not* get lost in the service of others, attempting to manage all the activity in front of you without a team to formulate a united plan.
- *Do* become clear on what you stand for and the space you are creating for others to build trust and flow.

While woman leadership suited Bea's genius because it's in summer phase (women leaders and networks have already formed and are now connecting), network marketing is in its autumn phase (people are already connected and seeking more trust and proof before acting). That meant Tamsine needed to take the lead with her Tempo Genius, which was a 180-degree shift from what they had been doing: Kevin had been leading with his Blaze Genius, running after the next opportunity with Tamsine chasing behind.

We took this transformation in their relationship as the model for their network to follow. Tamsine used her Tempo Genius to set a new tone and culture that grounded the network, with Kevin shining a light on it. While Blaze Geniuses tend to get focused on *what will be*, Tempo Geniuses are more focused on *what is right now*: not future fulfillment, but enjoying a fulfilling day right now, today. That became the identity for their new culture, and they brought their leaders together to plan a new way of leading things forward with a united schedule and rhythm.

Step Two: Master Your Market

- *Do not* get caught up in the minutiae of the market or in a market model that gets you stuck in daily activity that is not directly profitable.
- *Do* get a clear picture of who your market is and how you are delivering a superior service at the transactional level in a profitable way.

Tamsine and Kevin looked at their network and identified their top leaders, bringing them together for a session to share a vision of the future. They told their stories and recorded them as part of a document titled "The Network Effect," which laid out their vision in a way that was easy to share. They then looked at where their biggest networks were in South Africa to launch a pilot program for Network Dynamics and settled on a ten-week challenge in Cape Town.

The challenge would involve teams of eight on which each person would set ten-week goals in five areas of **WHERE** they wanted their life to be in ten weeks: **W**ealth, **H**ealth, **E**xcellence, **R**elationships, and **E**nvironment. They met once every week as a team all together in a weekly session run by Kevin to learn strategies and share successes.

With a plan in place, Tamsine's genius led the team to follow this rhythm. She collected the successes and challenges each week, connected people who could help each other, and tracked the growth of the teams. The program began with more than one hundred people and grew each week as the regular rhythm led to high energy and motivation throughout the entire network.

With a focus on the tangible benefit of being a part of their network, and with a focus on individual transformation and collective collaboration, their distributors found themselves attracting friends who wanted to join the program and, in turn, join the network.

Step Three: Monetize Your Moment
- *Do not* get lost in the activity and what you are doing now.
- *Do* start measuring things by the sales you are expecting.

Tempos like Tamsine always have a list of things to do and get caught up in that. At the end of the day, they've gone through the whole list but still haven't made any money. Monetizing her moment for Tamsine meant turning away from the to-do list and measuring everything based on her promotion: Did the promotion achieve the income they wanted and the expected result or did she need to fine-tune what they were doing? Was she getting the best results or did she need to change the way she was actually designing things to get a better result?

In their ten-week pilot project, there were three things Tamsine was measuring in their network: level of engagement (through feedback and success stories), new additions (through new registrations), and overall sales volume (through product purchases). Until Tamsine started measuring, they didn't feel they had much control over what they achieved each month. They just got busy and would receive a commission check each month. Now they were controlling their own measures and milestones and were far more motivated themselves, as were their leaders.

Over the ten weeks the program ran, they made sure everyone learned the three ways they could use their genius within their business: to manage themselves, to understand their customers, and to design their team leadership strategy. They had me share by video the four different strategies that fit the four geniuses to create a network effect (where people tell people and your network grows naturally and rapidly), and the team responded.

The Blaze Geniuses created weekly gatherings that were so much fun, the whole network invited their friends, who then joined their networks based on their experience at these events. The Steel

Geniuses did the opposite, creating a system that distributors could follow with one-to-one meetings every day. The Dynamo Genius leaders grew a uniquely different network based on adding creative content and material for their teams, whereas the Tempo Genius leaders grew a very different network that was not as "head in the clouds" and more "ear to the ground," focusing on the success stories and word-of-mouth instead of new innovations.

With Tamsine's Tempo Genius effortlessly handling the measures, Network 21 saw sales and new registrations more than double and engagement levels increase far beyond expectation (more than 80 percent wanted to take the program again). Everyone on the team had measurable wins and shifted their focus from the "closing sales" mentality of Orange Level to the "opening opportunities" mentality of Yellow Level.

The Dynamo Genius Path Out of Orange

What if you are a Dynamo in a job at Orange Level and want to move up? That was Heather Yelland's situation when I met her in 2011. She had been working in Australia with a well-known international speaker on a contract basis to mentor leaders in corporations. But she was now ready to create something of her own. She thought it would have to be something in her area of expertise (corporate consulting), but she didn't know exactly what. At the beginning of our mentoring, I asked her, "What would you want to be doing if you were no longer doing anything for the money?" She surprised both of us by saying, "I've always wanted to work with kids."

Heather dreamed of helping children with their education. But she saw it as something that would take time and focus, so she'd parked the idea in her mind for something later in life. I asked her how she would feel if she was transforming the lives of children *alongside* the businesses she was working with. She smiled, and we expanded the picture to include transformational mentoring of both company leaders and the world's future leaders: *our children.* Now she needed a personal identity: Instead of her going out and chasing new clients, she needed to stop and build a brand around who she was and attract them to her.

Step One: Identify Your Identity

- *Do not* keep on creating services or products based on your next best idea or your creative response to what each person is asking for.
- *Do* set up a clear identity for yourself that allows all your businesses, partnerships, and promotions to orbit around you.

Imagine you are five years in the future. You have achieved your success, and someone has written your entry on Wikipedia. What would you want the first paragraph to say? All successful leaders and entrepreneurs have one-paragraph summaries of who they are and what they stand for—and knew it themselves long before they became known for it. Knowing what you stand for is like establishing your position on the field in soccer: You choose and play that position, stay in that position, and make people want to pass the ball to you. You become *the opening for flow* instead of running anywhere you want to.

In other words, we turn on our winning formula when we choose to start doing one thing well. Heather walked through what she intuitively did with her corporate clients to bring them the results they wanted. She didn't have a product brand for it yet, but it became clear she had a step-by-step process she followed that took her to the heart of each enterprise. What were the emotions (not thoughts) that their cultures created in staff, partners, and customers? She would break these down and build them back up again from the heart. We came up with a brand name for this: Emotional Enterprise.

Step Two: Master Your Market

- *Do not* chase the business, constantly starting new things and knocking on doors hoping someone will buy what you're offering.
- *Do* connect with the people and partners who have models you can learn from and earn from, and get very clear on who is and is not your customer.

Mastering your market is not about trying to start something new without knowing what is already out there. It is about playing the game with those already on the field. Trying to master your market while chasing the business is like chasing butterflies. You might catch one every time you hunt, but you still need to go chasing them again tomorrow. Better to grow a garden where all the butterflies come to you every day. That's the key for a Dynamo: attraction. Dynamos need to use their natural creativity to focus *not* on *what* they are creating but on *how* they can get in front of the people who are their market from the moment they wake up.

Heather had done some research on exactly this point and was clear that she only wanted high-end corporate leaders to work with in her Emotional Enterprise business. But what about the young people she also wanted to help? She found that while student enrichment programs were in their infancy in Asia and Australia, they had been established in the United States for a long time. I shared with Heather my experience working with Joe Chapon and Bobbi Deporter on their SuperCamp program, which has become the world's leading summer enrichment program with twenty years of history.

Often, we will find that all our best learning to move to the next level comes from working with people who are already at that next level and learning from their models and their understanding of the market. This was true of Heather with Bobbi. SuperCamp programs give teenagers an immersive seven- and ten-day camp experience including life skills and accelerated learning skills. We had started running SuperCamps at Green School in Bali, but SuperCamps had not yet established a presence in Australia. Heather contacted Joe and set up a partnership to create a Super-Camp movement in Australia using all the tools and structures Joe and Bobbi had already put in place working with more than one million children all over the world.

Now Heather just needed a better way to reach the market in Australia than knocking on doors. She had to think about the people who were waking up each day wanting the best for their children and would want to come to an Australian SuperCamp: Where were they? Who were the people who were already out in front of them that could be her potential partners to connect with those parents? What would be the simplest and easiest way to make sure her message was in front of them?

Step Three: Monetize Your Moment

- *Do not* just open your doors and hope for the money to walk in.
- *Do* create promotions focused on bringing a specific amount of business in a specific time frame, with enough time to test and measure your assumptions each day, and learn your way to earn.

Dynamo Geniuses are always tempted to start new things without finishing the things we have started, which is why we can often fail to monetize our moments even when we have found the markets to master. We'd rather run around and create more things instead of zeroing in on very specific promotions, testing and measuring them, and finding smarter and better ways to do them. When we do that, even if we don't get the business that we want, we learn what is working and what is not.

When we set a promotion, we set a destination and attract the people who want to get to that same destination. We gather the support we need with many willing to get the reward and collectively achieve the result. That is the key behind monetizing the moment: getting to the point where you can keep on improving and growing your business with a team and eventually take bigger bets on the size of the promotions that you can run and the size of the partners that you can work with. That is *the* really big step when we move from knowing we have positive cash coming in to constructing the market flow for our enterprises to expanding them or moving on to other businesses. Once we learn how everything connects, we can really control the flow—a very different feeling from showing up and hoping the business comes in the door.

Heather learned from the promotions that the US SuperCamp team and our team in Bali were already running. She ran a scholarship promotion through parents and students, which spread virally. With education a hot topic in Australia, she established SuperCamp as a solution for providing accelerated learning skills and generated media attention. That attention in turn earned her the opportunity to speak about SuperCamp on stage at events and conferences.

The result was that Heather attracted not only registrations for her first camp but also clients for her Emotional Enterprise business. Instead of it being difficult to follow her mission and follow the money at the same time, as she had thought in the past, she now found that it was actually *easier* to attract business by being true to herself and making a stand for what she believed in and the difference she wanted to make.

With the added business, it has also been easier to grow the camps, with Heather's corporate connections sponsoring student scholarships. Because Heather didn't want to get stuck in the detail, she maintained the SuperCamp model, adjusting it to fit the Australian market. She learned what size team she needed, what her break-even point was, and what activities she should and should not be focused on.

Heather now understands what all geniuses do when they move up from Orange to Yellow Level: Once you have identified your identity and mastered your market, you are likely to find that there are ways to connect with others where you can be of value to them and learn from them without needing to work it all out yourself. Your value is someone else's leverage, so there is always a way to play with others.

Spectator Versus Player

This book may be called *Millionaire Master Plan*, and indeed your goal may be to make millions. But that may not be your goal at all. Perhaps you are simply looking for peace of mind in your career or job to provide for your family without the stress of chasing every dollar. Perhaps you would be happy just having the security to know you are not dependent on the job you have; you'd be financially fine without it.

This is the point of moving up the Wealth Lighthouse: It is not about roles like employed or self-employed, owner or investor, poor or rich; it's about having this choice and control over your financial future. This makes climbing from Orange to Yellow Level a critical point in your climb, because you are going to not just another level but another prism. The Foundation Prism is where most of us reside today, but the Enterprise Prism is where all the money is made. That's where the real action is.

Think of the difference between the Foundation and Enterprise Prisms—between Orange Worker and Yellow Player—as a major sporting event like a soccer match. There are many, many more spectators (yes, even in America) than there are people playing the game. Those who remain spectators are like those at Infrared and Red Levels—largely anonymous and able to come and go as they please. The game does not depend on them, and they don't have to follow many rules to be there other than not to drink too much and to stay off the field. Spectators rarely move from their seats, but they are extremely vocal. They have strong opinions on the successes and failures of the players on the field and shout their advice to the players, the referee, and anyone who will listen.

If you have made it to Orange Level, you have earned the right to stop being a spectator and get onto the field with the players. The players are known and recognized for their overall skill and how they play their positions. They are expected to train for the game, be good at it, and follow the rules to compete. Everyone, especially the spectators, has high expectations and holds them accountable for the results of the game.

If you think of Orange Workers as spectators in the stands, Yellow Players as the players on the field, and the ball as money, opportunity, or resources, you can see why no one is passing you that ball yet: You're not on the field playing the game. That is the biggest challenge for entrepreneurs and those of us in jobs at Orange Level. If you start a business or stay in a job to get in the game and then just end up chasing the money, that's like a spectator running on the field trying to chase the ball. No one wants to play with you, and you never catch up with the ball anyway.

So why are so many people in the world spectators rather than players in the Wealth Lighthouse? *Because our education system has been focused on taking the step from Red to Orange*: **How to turn us from Red Survivors dependent on our parents or government to Orange Workers working hard to keep a job.**

Yet everyone I know at Orange Level is fearful they won't have an income in the future. That's the reason the positive feelings of creating value and accomplishment with your job at Orange Level are mixed with worry that if you lose your job it will be tough to find another one. That worry is also there if you are self-employed:

You are always dependent on chasing the next contract and keeping the current ones going to maintain your cash flow.

But everyone I know at Yellow Level, whether they are employed or self-employed, business owners or investors, has no fear of losing their incomes or their jobs. Yellow Players have simply learned the essential extra skill of creating their own jobs, so they are always getting offers of employment or business. They have followed the three steps out of Orange Level and moved from dependent to independent. When you move to Yellow Level, you have freedom to move when you want to from one job or contract to another. You have stepped over the wall separating the stands from the field and are serious about playing the game.

In other words, you no longer have to chase the soccer ball all the time even when you are on the field, because you have a team in other positions to do that. As a result, you spend less time running around and more time getting into the flow of the game and moving where you could be of most value. By being in those places, you actually get the ball passed to you more often.

To do this most effectively, however, you need to choose a position, train, show up, and be accountable in a very different way than you do as just a spectator. Having a ticket and a seat is no longer enough to succeed; you have to master your part of the game, and this requires *three important practices that run contrary to what most of us learned at school*:

1. **Learning comes from action: To know and not to do is not yet to know.** Mastery at Yellow Level does not come from reading a book but from practice; the learning comes from the doing. At school, we are taught to be book smart. To be a wealth creator, you need to be street smart. Wealth creators need to do in order to know. Take action and then learn from it. *That's why this book is more than a book: It is*

a gateway to a series of Playbooks at every level that you can access and complete online to make sure you're playing the right game by the right rules.

2. **Learning is a game: That means it must be fun, and you need to know the rules.** Choosing the right game to play and the right position to learn in that game is essential at this point: It must be a game that naturally suits your genius so you enjoy it and keep playing with enjoyment, because the more you play it, the better you get.

3. **Success comes from effective giving: You don't score by getting the ball; you score by passing it on.** Too many of us worry about passing on ideas or opportunities because we think they won't come back. Think of a baseball game where the ball gets hit into the crowd: It never comes back. But the ball always stays in play when we focus on giving. Ineffective giving is when you pass to the spectators. Effective giving is when you pass to other players on the field. Even if the competition takes it now and then, the ball stays in play, which means what you pass eventually ends up getting passed back.

That's the key now that you are moving to Yellow Level, effective giving: being in the right place for others *to pass the ball to you* and for you then *to pass it on*. In this way, as we pass on opportunities, resources, and money, everyone on the field gets to kick the ball many times. We end up winning together.

That's the fulfilling nature of flow we experience in the Enterprise Prism when we let go and reach Yellow Level instead of holding on at Orange.

CHAPTER FIVE SUMMARY

- **Orange Level is the final Foundation Prism level.** When you are at Orange Level, you are in positive cash flow but still dependent on others. To move to Yellow Level is moving from dependence to independence.

- **All flow is made up of projects and processes.** Projects grow or enhance flow. Processes maintain flow. All successful wealth creators in the Enterprise Prism have mastered how to automate or outsource their processes, so they can focus all their time on profitable projects: promotions.

- **Your rise up the Wealth Lighthouse comes from the Power of Zero.** As you move up each level of the Wealth Lighthouse, what feels like a little and a lot of money changes—in general by a factor of ten. Don't stretch yourself with a $10,000 promotion if you haven't yet mastered $1,000 promotions.

- **There is a Wealth Equation: Wealth = Value × Leverage.** Value exchange creates speed of money flow. Leveraging value increases volume of money flow. Between these two variables, rivers of wealth are created.

- **There are three steps to Yellow Level:**

  Identify Your Identity
  Master Your Market
  Monetize Your Moment

- **Orange Workers are like spectators at a soccer game.** There are three important practices allowing them to stop watching the game and move to Yellow:

  1. Learning comes from action.
  2. Learning is a game, which means it must be fun and you need to know the rules.
  3. Success comes from effective giving—passing on, not holding on.

Preflight Checklist: Yellow Level

Your personal page on www.millionairemasterplan.com has supplemental guides and videos, including assessments and Playbooks, for each of the checklist points below. I have included one of the exercises from the Playbook at the end of this chapter: the anatomy of a promotion.

Being clear on your position and how you relate to your market puts you on the map. These are the steps to convert your time into money and tap into the flow of the markets. Complete the checklist now: Tick yes or no. How do you rate? When all nine are checked yes, you will have connected your personal passion and purpose to your Flight Path.

Identify Your Identity

1. I have a clear path to my ideal identity with role models
   to follow and a clear identity today that I can express.   ☐ Yes   ☐ No

2. I have a reputation in my niche as a distinct leader in
   my field who creates attraction in business and
   opportunities.   ☐ Yes   ☐ No

3. I have aligned all my actions, messaging, and marketing
   to reflect clearly my identity to my market and
   the world.   ☐ Yes   ☐ No

Master Your Market

1. I have sized my market; I know my competitors and
   what my unique market position and market share are
   and will be.   ☐ Yes   ☐ No

2. I have segmented my market and designed my time and
   business around the different needs of my customers.   ☐ Yes   ☐ No

3. I have systems and a rhythm that keep me close to my
   customers, my competitors, and the market shapers.   ☐ Yes   ☐ No

Monetize Your Moment

1. I have outsourced or automated all my business
   processes so I can focus on profitable promotions. ☐ Yes ☐ No

2. I have an annual schedule of promotion plans that
   links to my monthly profit-and-loss and cash
   flow forecasts. ☐ Yes ☐ No

3. I have aligned my team and partners to a weekly
   rhythm of results, testing, and measuring based
   on our promotions. ☐ Yes ☐ No

ACTION POINT

The DNA of a Great Promotion

All promotions have the same structure and the same principles of design. From small launch promotions for new retail or service companies to online promotions and new product promotions to capital-raising promotions and multimillion-dollar property promotions, they all follow the same underlying principle: *the golden thread*.

The following steps are a summary adapted from the Monetize Your Moment Playbook you will find online. Use these steps to set up your promotion plan and golden thread.

Before you begin, remember four things:

1. This is the third step to Yellow Level in the Wealth Lighthouse. It presupposes each promotion is aligned to your identity and within your market.
2. Whatever your assumptions are, *you will be wrong*. Things will *always* be better or worse than you think. You will constantly be off from week to week and need to course-correct. Making those simple adjustments will get you back

on course, provided you are checking against your plan regularly with your team.

3. Every promotion has a plan, a profit, and a time frame and is a dance between you and your market. Every action by you leads to a reaction by your market, so you need to measure every step and adjust as necessary. Like turning on a tap, great leaders learn how to increase the amount they can generate in a promotion one zero at a time (from $1,000 to $10,000, and $10,000 to $100,000). For money to flow, they know they need to learn what the market values and ensure value trumps cost every time.

4. Your ability to attract partners and investors as you move up the Wealth Lighthouse will depend on your track record in setting milestones and delivering on them in your promotions. That's how you build trust within your market. And it all begins with your first promotion.

Your Promotion Plan

Name: What is the name of your promotion?
Leader: Who will lead and be responsible for this promotion?

Why: The Purpose

Why is this promotion important now? Is it developing a new product? Is it adding new systems to the business? Is it building your brand in the market?

What: The Objectives

Limit your key objectives to three areas:

- **Financial Objectives:** What are the specific revenue and profit targets?

- **Development Objectives:** What are the ongoing revenue streams, new products, systems, markets, or teams that will result from this promotion?
- **Learning Objectives:** What new learning and expertise will you uncover?

Who: Team Members

List each person on the team and his or her area of responsibility.

When: Time Frame and Milestones

Create a simple schedule of milestones from beginning to end: Start Date, Completion Date, and Weekly Team Review Date & Time.

Date	Milestones	Revenue
Week 1		
Week 2		
Week 3		

How: Promotion Strategy

- What is your irresistible offer?
- Who is your market?
- What is the budget you are redirecting?
- What problem are you solving?
- Why is your solution superior?
- What is the urgency to buy now?
- What is the pain of missing out?
- What is your price and promotion?

Promotion: Your Golden Thread

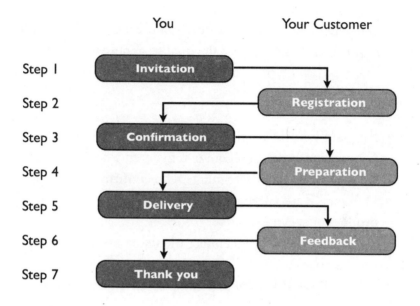

All great promotions follow the same seven steps with each step measurable and controllable:

1. A Compelling Invitation: What is it? Who will it reach? When and how?
2. Simple Registration: Automated, measurable, trackable
3. A Firm Confirmation: Building commitment, immediate payoff
4. Thoughtful Preparation: Building anticipation, setting expectations
5. High-Impact Delivery: Exceed expectations, make a new invitation
6. Easy Feedback: Honest reflection, quantifiable improvement
7. A Sincere Thank-You: Completion of the promotion, an enchanted end

Capture each step in your promotion with your marketing material, emails, presentation material, and any documentation that you can refer back to in the future. Compare how you and your team perform at every step with best practices and the metrics in your industry. By improving the quality and flow of your interaction at every level, you can measure the impact at every step of the golden thread:

- Registration Rate (percentage invited who register)
- Conversion Rate (percentage registered who buy)
- Engagement Rate (percentage who confirm or prepare)
- Delivery Rate (percentage who buy who receive the full product or service)
- Satisfaction Rate (percentage of customers who give positive feedback)
- Repurchase Rate (percentage of customers who make another purchase)

PART III

THE ENTERPRISE PRISM AND BEYOND

Level 4—Yellow Level: Player
Level 5—Green Level: Performer
Level 6—Blue Level: Conductor

Mastering these levels leads to a connection to the wealth flowing through our markets: our ability to add value and leverage the value of others through businesses and assets.

It isn't money that makes money. It's people who make money.
And it's other people who will help you make your money.

FROM YELLOW TO GREEN: PLAYER TO PERFORMER

Measure:	Positive cash flow from mastering your market
Emotions:	Self-reliance; attraction; limitation
Cost of staying here:	Limited growth; limited impact; isolation
Focus needed:	Rhythm and mastery
How did I get here?	Resourcefulness; resilience; stubbornness
How do I move up?	Establish Your Enterprise; Refine Your Rhythm; Synchronize Your Steps

Welcome to the Enterprise Prism, where all the money is made. You have mastered the Foundation Prism. Whether you are in a business, are self-employed, or hold a job, you find yourself in demand. There's money coming in and opportunities everywhere. You are a Player now. You love what you do and create your own flow. As a result, you could live out your life happily on this level, but you also have earned the right to let your genius take initiative and shine even brighter.

Be careful, though: Yellow Level can become a vortex of

frustration. You can easily get stuck and achieve only a fraction of your true potential. Many find their winning formula here by putting the "pedal to the metal." They believe the more they apply themselves, the more they can achieve. The result is multiple projects or businesses, all of them moving but none of them really working as well as they should. *That's because they all depend on the same thing: you. And if you stop, the money stops.*

This is called the Octopus Effect: On the surface, it looks like you or your business is successful because you have money coming in and so much going on; beneath the surface, there are many tentacles relying on one small brain, and everything sucks.

Overcoming the Octopus Effect

The shift from this octopus-like Yellow Player Level (in which one person does all things) to Green Performer Level (where all people do one thing) *does not* happen by putting your foot on the accelerator. Instead, you take your foot off the accelerator, put it on the clutch, and change gears.

This means doing the opposite of the winning formula that got you to Yellow Level. It's why Green Level is counterintuitive for someone at Yellow, as it appears you are giving up your freedom. But this is less about freedom and more about responsibility to something greater than you. That's why it is a myth that you need to leave your job and start your own business (see Vaughn Clair's Steel Genius story that follows) or spend all your nights and weekends trying to invest in property or shares in order to create more wealth.

If you are in a job but want to start your own path, don't see the job as a limit to the financial growth you are seeking; see it as an education in which you are getting paid. All large organizations and corporations are at Green Level and do not rely on any one person. The skills you learn in how to work within a team are invaluable for when you build your own organization. So you *can* move from Orange to Yellow to Green Level while working with others, following your genius, and avoiding the Octopus.

In fact, I try to make sure of it with my own team, and so do many others who know the advantages to moving their team members up the Wealth Lighthouse. For example, Suraj Naik started with me straight out of college and went from Orange to Yellow to Green Level, where he is now, leading the development of my Entrepreneurs Institute online platform, GeniusU.

He has a team that manages all aspects of the business while he leads them as a Blaze Genius. But the key moment for him was when he learned to slow down at Yellow Level and focus less on driving the business himself and more on dividing up the thinking and actions to create a model and rhythm where everyone on his team was empowered and responsible to do their own thing. This is a key step for a Green Performer.

As a result, during our busiest time of the year in 2013, while we were implementing all our new systems, Suraj was still able to take a long-planned trip to Europe with his friends, jumping out of planes and returning having achieved one of his dreams: his skydiving qualification. If he had been working like an octopus, trying to manage everything by himself, he would have had more worry and less time—and that would've "sucked."

In truth, Suraj's example of achieving Green Level while working for someone else only partially underscores one of five myths of wealth that keep people from moving beyond Yellow Level.

The Five Modern Myths of Wealth

Why do so many people seeking wealth creation get it wrong, rushing into "solutions" without first mastering the skills needed? *Because in the last few decades, we have been taught things about wealth that are not or are no longer true.* In all my mentoring of thousands of wealth creators in countries all over the world, the first challenge for most of them is unlearning the five biggest myths of wealth in order to ascend farther in the Wealth Lighthouse:

1. Wealth Comes from Passive Income

- **Myth:** You can get wealthy by going into debt to buy assets that will give you passive income so you no longer have to work for a living.
- **Truth:** You've just dug a hole, not a river. All income needs to be managed, which means you need to know how to manage a team and experts who can manage your portfolio of assets.

Yes, building assets that create cash flow is a critical part of building your wealth. But many people have been burned by stretching their resources to buy property or other assets in the hope that they will yield ongoing passive income, only to see the value of their assets drop, their cash flow go negative, and their credit ratings ruined. Why didn't this happen to all the wealthiest people? The wealthiest people know all their assets—whether properties or business—need to be managed well. There's nothing passive about it.

It might look like the apple farmer has "passive income" because his apple trees keep giving him apples, but it still takes time and expertise to nurture those trees. It's the same with your assets: Choose assets with great care and factor in the true cost of choosing, managing, and selling your assets in your return.

Replace the myth of passive income with the reality of portfolio income, where each of your assets is part of a portfolio managed by a team. Monitor and maintain your portfolio and the return it is giving you.

2. *Wealth Comes From Multiple Streams of Income*

- **Myth:** The more income streams you can start, the wealthier you will become.
- **Truth:** Starting many streams at the same time is like trying to push many balls up a hill at the same time: You may get started, but you end up losing your focus and your time. Success comes from growing teams, not streams: multiple *teams* of income.

This myth is perhaps the most destructive in the Foundation Prism—but it's dangerous at any level. If everyone around you is unclear what your main focus is—what your position is and where you stand on the field—you will constantly chase the ball instead of having it kicked to you.

What people must learn by Yellow Level and take to Green Level is that money doesn't make money; *people* make money. Invest in the right people before investing in the assets they will manage or you will be the one doing all the juggling, and it will only be a matter of time before you start dropping the ball.

3. *Wealth Comes From Your Exit Strategy*

- **Myth:** Wealth comes when you sell out: Plan an exit strategy where you can work hard now and earn the money later.
- **Truth:** Keep working, because you love what you do. Don't strive to bake a pie so you can sell it; own the bakery so you can bake as many pies as you want, sell some, and keep the rest.

I have met too many people who are holding out for an exit that will make it all worth it. They don't enjoy what they are doing. They have simply talked themselves into grinning and bearing it

"until I make X dollars or until I sell the company for X amount."
Sure, we hear stories of people cashing out with big returns from
their businesses or assets, but rarely do these stories involve people
not passionate about what they were doing.

Replace the myth of an *exit* strategy (leaving the game) with a
success strategy (staying in the game). The wealthiest people in the
world are still doing what they are doing because it doesn't feel like
hard work following your genius and doing what you love. As you
move up to Blue Level, any exit strategies are not for you; they are
for your project partners and investors.

4. Wealth Comes From Being Your Own Boss

- **Myth:** The path to wealth begins by being your own boss
  and choosing what you do and when you do it.
- **Truth:** Wealth comes not from being your own boss but
  from choosing who your boss will be.

The truth is, we all remain accountable to someone, whether
it is our customers, shareholders, or teams. Being your own boss
means you have just put the one person in charge of you who is the
least able to hold you accountable: *you*. It is a lonely path.

I always select the right person to lead every plan, project, and
business I start *and* my part in it. That means I have someone to
whom I am accountable. I have the freedom to choose who is the
boss of me for everything I want to be involved in. I just make
sure I establish a rhythm to check in on how they are doing and
what I need to do to support them that ensures I remain of service,
accountable, and connected to them.

5. Wealth Comes From Risking It All

- **Myth:** The hero's journey is the nature of entrepreneurship
  and comes from putting everything on the line for your big
  idea. Big risks achieve big rewards.

- **Truth:** From climbing Mount Everest to going to the moon, the most heroic journeys are the ones that minimize risk; the ones in which you progress deliberately, testing and measuring each step before you take it to stay on the path to success.

There are two types of failure: those that steer you and those that sink you. Climbing the Wealth Lighthouse has its risks: The higher you climb, the farther you have to fall. So the higher you climb, the more you need to prepare. Replace the myth of *risking it all* with the reality of *minimizing your risk to experience it all*.

Taken together, the five myths are a mechanical way of thinking about wealth, separating us all into paths where we're trying to do it all on our own. The truths are a more natural way in which building assets is replaced by growing flow, where we are all connected to each other and the market. In flow, everything is connected, and your role in nurturing, enhancing, and expanding the flow around you is more important than trying to work out how to make the money and exit the game.

Still skeptical these are myths? Pick up any "Richest People" list and ask yourself for each successful wealth creator on it:

- Are they passive in their income or very active?
- Are they trying to create multiple streams or do they have multiple teams creating the streams?
- Are they following an exit strategy or a success strategy?
- Are they only accountable to themselves or to others around them?
- Are they risking it all or taking measured risks to test and measure?

Once you clear your mind of these myths, you're ready to step up and through the Enterprise Prism. That starts by taking the three steps to move up from Yellow.

The Three Steps From Yellow to Green

As we go through these steps, keep in mind two truths. First, *you do not need to run your own business* to create the necessary attraction, income, and security to move up a level. You can do it by upgrading your job. Second, if you are self-employed, you can move to Green Level by *following the three steps within your existing business*. Many people do find it much easier to design a new Green Level business alongside their Yellow Level business, but you can use your Superman Time to build a Green Level team in your own business, while you keep the cash flowing at Yellow with your Clark Kent Time!

The following stories have examples of these choices. But remember: This is a choice now. You may be at Yellow Level and be quite happy running a small business with the freedom to do what you want when you want. That's okay! But if you find it more appealing to have a company that works without you, and eventually to have teams managing your multiple streams of income, you will need to follow these three steps to Green Level.

1. **Establish Your Enterprise:** Yellow Players identify their identities by creating businesses that revolve around their geniuses. Green Performers establish their enterprise by creating businesses that can work without them. Your businesses must have different financial models that can afford strong leadership teams. They must have their own missions and models that do not need to include you, with a schedule of multiple promotions that your teams can manage.

2. **Refine Your Rhythm:** The freedom you had to do what you want when you wanted at Yellow Level changes to a pre-organized rhythm that everyone can follow at Green. In other words, you move from lead guitar to drummer, where you improvise less and instead set the rhythm for the team and

create a level of trust and communication that every high-performing team needs. This means scheduling the year ahead of time: Milestones, measures, and meetings are set to review and renew. (There is a rhythm to how you review and renew everything from your overall strategy to your promotions, policies, and operations; this is summarized at the end of this chapter and in detail in the Refine Your Rhythm Playbook on www.millionairemasterplan.com.)

3. **Synchronize Your Steps:** Yellow Players can make it up as they go. Green Performers need to plan ahead of time: all people doing one thing instead of one person doing all things. You synchronize the steps the team takes with the "seasons" it needs to navigate from the growth of spring to winter, when everything changes and slows before moving toward renewal.

Each genius has a different way to create value and leverage the value of others through these steps. Read Scott Picken's Blaze path first, where I cover the three big excuses that stop every genius from moving up to Green Level and go into greater detail on how the three steps overcome those excuses. Then go ahead and read your own genius path, but do study the others to understand how other geniuses on the teams you build need to think.

The Blaze Path From Yellow to Green

Scott Picken is a South African entrepreneur based in Cape Town. He has been the South African representative for Tony Robbins and Chet Holmes's Business Breakthroughs and built an international property business investing in Australian property. When I met Scott several years ago, he took the Wealth Spectrum test and came out at Yellow Level.

"I've had enough of doing it myself," he said. "Show me how

to move up to Green Level." I became Scott's mentor, but before I could help him take the three steps up, I needed to confront the excuses that he and *every Yellow Level Player* make that stop them from climbing farther in the Wealth Lighthouse.

- **I can't find people who can do it like me.** Used by Yellow Level leaders who convince themselves that only they can get the job done, because they have not invested the time to ensure new leaders succeed.
- **I can't afford good people.** Used when Yellow Level entrepreneurs have not invested the time to create a financial model enabling them to afford good leadership. Even if they could find good people, they couldn't afford to bring them on.
- **I'm too busy to find and train the right people.** Used by Yellow Level players who have no time because they have designed a world that revolves around their own importance; the only constant is busy-ness.

I gave Scott these three excuses and asked him which one applied to him. Scott laughed and said, "All three."

As I've said before, we stay at any level because there's something we're not prepared to let go of to move up. I asked Scott if he was ready to give up the one thing that he valued most that had gotten him to Yellow Level. Scott asked what that was, and I replied, "*Freedom.*"

At Yellow Level, we love being free to change our minds and do what we want, when we want. Yellow Level is all about you being in the limelight and being significant. The idea of having to report in to your business with more discipline and to keep to a plan and schedule feels like a step backward. But without a rhythm that allows a team to get into harmony and high performance, you'll never set the team up for success.

Green Level is all about you supporting your team to be significant. It's about empowering others to worry about your business even more than you do. Once you have earned the right to a higher level of freedom in the Enterprise Prism—Blue Level, where you have multiple teams and multiple streams—you'll get your freedom back with a far higher level of flow attached to it.

Scott heard me and made the commitment to confront all of his excuses.

His first excuse came because he had designed his business to work around him, without clear, documented roles, expectations, or measures that someone else could assume. It was impossible for someone else to come in and take over his role. To overcome this hurdle, we broke down his role into a number of jobs that he could find people to do better than he could. Then we created a new niche that would attract people to his business instead of to him, which I'll cover shortly.

His second excuse came because he had designed a cost model that earned him a living but had no margin and budget for leadership. We redesigned his business model so there was enough money to pay for good people.

His third excuse came because he had designed his time so he had none left to train others even if he wanted to. We redesigned his schedule so he could have time with his family and to travel, while growing his business.

Within twelve months, Scott went from struggling with three badly run businesses to one multimillion-dollar business run well. He knew he needed to change, and he did so by following his Blaze Genius path from Yellow to Green Level.

Step One: Establish Your Enterprise

- *Do not* keep up the excuses that you are the only one who can lead the business and continue to come up with strategies that only you can execute.

- *Do* establish your enterprise revolving around a team with strong leaders in the other three geniuses developing the overall strategy, standards, policies, processes, and financial management while you lead from the front, using your genius to shine a light on the success of your team.

The first step for Blazes at Green Level is to give their enterprises a stronger identity than themselves and get clear about what size of flow they plan to see three years from now:

- What market position?
- How many customers?
- What revenue and profit?
- What value will it deliver customers?
- What market value will the company have?
- What size and quality team?
- What financial systems do you need?
- What culture, service, training, partnerships, and communications?

The next step is to set up the projects to support that flow. This sounds overwhelming at Yellow Level—you are used to working everything out yourself. But at Green Level, you have a team to deal with the answers.

For Scott, we began by rethinking his entire market. Blaze Geniuses have a tendency to be distracted by new opportunities and relationships that come their way. To move to Green, Scott redirected this Blaze energy internally to focus first on his best customers, his team, and a plan.

He began by evaluating what would be the most attractive country to be investing in. Many of Scott's clients had stopped investing with him when the Australian property market stalled. Scott went back to the top 5 percent of his clients and asked them what their criteria would be to make them reinvest with him. He compared that with different property markets around the world and decided to focus on the US market.

Scott then designed a business model that would allow him to pay for a leadership team, property partners in the United States, and a sales team in South Africa. *From day one, he would have a model that could work without him.*

Step Two: Refine Your Rhythm

- *Do not* work within your own time frame, operating your business and your life without a clear proactive schedule of promotions.
- *Do* set a rhythm that empowers the team, keeps you in check, and manages you as much as it manages the business.

Once Scott had set the new direction for his company, he set up a plan for how much of his time he would be in South Africa and how much in the United States, worked out who he needed on his team, and determined how they would all measure their success.

By his first visit to the United States, he already had soft commitments from clients on what they would be willing to invest in. That helped him narrow down to the right partners there who could locate the investment properties for him. Just six months after starting this process, using his Blaze connecting ability but letting the team do the other work, he had his first deals completed.

The team then took the company's goals for the year and turned them into promotions, with a number of investor conferences in South Africa and a number of investor trips to the United States. Not Scott—the *team*. Like most Blaze Geniuses, Scott will always be overly optimistic on what people can achieve, which is great to inspire them short-term but not so good in motivating them long-term if the targets are unrealistic. When Scott took his Blaze Genius out of the equation, the team reset their targets based on what they could confidently stretch to achieve rather than what Scott wanted them to achieve.

The result? The team found new, more innovative ways to reach their sales targets that worked for each of their geniuses, and they stepped up to take on system development and financial management roles that Scott had been struggling with on his own. Having been given more authority to drive things at their pace, team members went out of their way to find ways to free Scott's time up so he could spend his time connecting with their top clients and staying in his flow.

The team now had a rhythm—a new pace and clarity—which led to step three.

Step Three: Synchronize Your Steps

- *Do not* keep pushing things at your pace regardless of the market conditions or state of your team (thus pushing them to the breaking point).
- *Do* align your team and your plan with the rhythm of the markets and of your industry, pacing your growth to synchronize with the flow of the markets, industry, and activities of your partners.

With a new focus, new business model, and motivated team, Scott began building his leadership and sales teams to manage the flow that had now started. He designed the yearly cycle of the business to synchronize with the seasonal shifts in the markets. He worked out who was needed for the different positions in the business and the strengths they would need. He designed his own time so that he could be in the business at the critical moments when he was most needed.

The team then planned the timing of their US trips to coincide with most investors' availability to travel and set their conference schedules to maximize attendance. They developed partnerships in South Africa and the United States to support their marketing and the quality of property investments they made available to their clients. This allowed them to focus on being able to test and measure the most effective ways to match the right clients to the right investments.

In the meantime, Scott was freed up to stay in his flow, investing his time with their top clients and generating more income for the company and more cash flow for himself, while the team ran the company.

It wasn't long before the flow grew far beyond what Scott had been achieving with the Australian market. A year after confronting all his excuses, Scott was growing a new business in a new country, beating his own sales targets, and energizing an entirely fresh base of investors in South Africa with business growing rapidly just by word-of-mouth. Most important, he was taking actions where he felt in control of the results and no longer needed to chase the business in order to grow it.

The Tempo Path From Yellow to Green

While Blaze Geniuses should take roles within their businesses that bring out their strengths in communication and marketing to others, Tempo Geniuses get into their flow fastest when taking roles in service or trading. That means they are looking for others to lead the business while they keep their ear to the ground. This is exactly what my wife, Renate, did in her business as we increased our cash flow and moved into Yellow Level promotions.

We had moved from $6,400 to $12,800 in positive cash flow by setting up a holding company that billed each of our businesses for our services. This helped Renate, a self-employed real estate agent, as her commissions came in irregularly. By billing Expat Rentals for her time each month, she turned cash flow from a personal problem into a business problem, where she could focus on making the sales to cover overheads.

To get us to Green Level, I moved first in my publishing and conference businesses, organizing my companies to work without me. Renate was next, first with Expat Rentals in Singapore and then with Vision Villas in Bali. Here's what Renate stopped and started doing to move her business to Green.

Step One: Establish Your Enterprise

- *Do not* get so busy with day-to-day activity that you can't set aside the time to assemble the team and set a higher mission and stronger model for your business.
- *Do* use your sensory skills to select the right Blaze Genius to take on communications and marketing, a Dynamo Genius to create the strategy, and the right Steel Genius to manage the financials of your business with you keeping things balanced.

To move from Yellow to Green Levels requires your business to have more attraction than you do. Your company also needs to be number one in something, and if it isn't yet big enough to be number one, narrow your niche until it can be. Renate set a focus for Expat Rentals to have a niche in rentals of $3,000 and above, which was the high-end market in Singapore.

With attraction in her niche marketplace growing from both agents who co-brokered with her and from clients who found us through my publishing company's sister publication, *Expat Living*, Renate attracted two very capable managers from friends she met through her mom's network. This is the strength of Tempo Geniuses: They are great at building strong relationships. Deborah Law became the general manager of Expat Rentals, and Rebecca Bisset became the editor and publisher of the magazine *Expat Living*.

By the time we moved from Singapore to Bali, both Rebecca and Deborah were leading the two companies profitably. Today the two companies continue to grow in Singapore.

In the meantime, with Expat Rentals moving from Yellow to Green Level, Renate had time to build another business that suited her strengths. When we moved to Bali and found our dream resort, Renate took the reins in leading the management of the staff. First, she established our enterprise with a unique identity, "Vision Villas." The resort would become a social enterprise connected to the John Fawcett Foundation, which was giving cataract surgeries to Balinese to restore their eyesight.

As a workshop retreat, Vision Villas became a place to get vision and give vision. This focus on personal and leadership development made it stand out against the many other resorts on the island. Renate now focused on the resort's next step.

Step Two: Refine Your Rhythm

- *Do not* get so caught up in your daily routine that you fail to set a long-term rhythm for your team or set a strategy that allows the team to support and grow the business.
- *Do* treat your position within your enterprise as one part to play: Be ruthless in saying no to the things you're not so strong at and yes to delivering the service standards, maintaining the culture, and keeping the balance within the company.

Yellow Players tend to create complex businesses that revolve around their unique abilities. Moving to Green Level means simplifying the business model so it is easier for leaders who are familiar with that model to run it.

That was the case with our resort, and as I mentioned earlier, Renate used her experience from a previous job—working as part of a team in a Green Level environment of a hospital from our days in London—to set her up for success. Once Renate focused on how we would deliver our services, we set up a series of promotions to fill the resort, giving ourselves the comfort that we would have the cash flow when we opened. We then hired managers far more experienced than either of us who knew how to run resorts, starting with a general manager, Wayan Suarma, who in turn hired his finance head, operations head, and front office head; they in turn hired the rest of the staff.

Renate then set a weekly schedule where she could check on the details—the Tempo strength—while letting the team run and grow the resort. This led to her third step.

Step Three: Synchronize Your Steps

- *Do not* get caught up in the day-to-day where you are spending most of your time being reactive to the things around you and changing plans as you go.
- *Do* take the time to set a strategy and pace so that you are always one step ahead and able to make the most of the market trends.

Without synchronizing your steps, your business cannot surf with the wave of the market. But Tempo Geniuses should *not* be leading the strategy of a business. That is not their strength. Having others set the strategy that you can push back on, question, and fine-tune is a far more effective path forward for your genius and the entire team. This allows you to use your sensory acuity to tune in to a clear plan that links your business to the market.

Both Renate's businesses evolved as the market evolved. As more expats began buying property in Singapore, Expat Rentals became Expat Realtor and extended its reach from rentals to sales. As the entrepreneur market grew, Vision Villas evolved from a workshop retreat to an entrepreneur resort running one-month accelerator programs for entrepreneurs.

The most important part of doing this goes beyond Green: Yellow Level businesses cannot be easily sold, as they are dependent on the Player; Green Level businesses build capital value, which means you can sell part or all of the business when and if needed. Understanding this is to understand how assets grow—and how they are bought and sold—and it moves you to Blue Level and beyond.

By taking this interest in the ebb and flow of the market, with the skill of knowing how to build and grow a team, Renate and I learned together in our businesses the importance of synchronizing our steps. Too often, one partner would evolve, leaving the other behind. By growing together through our own geniuses, we understood each other's journey and how to weather the changes and challenges together.

As I have said earlier, moving up the spectrum doesn't solve all your problems. Renate and I still have challenges. Scott still has challenges. But as you rise up the levels, these bigger challenges come with more resources to address them. As you rise up each level, you also spot more resources so you don't get stuck waiting for what you don't have: You become more *resourceful*.

The Steel Path From Yellow to Green

At some point, being a Yellow Player is simply not enough, especially if the industry you are in is changing. When I met Vaughn Clair, he was near the end of the line in his business. He had spent his life installing complicated point-of-sale systems in large companies, first in a job and then on his own through contract work. When I met him in 2012, his last contract, with the Australia Post, was coming to an end, as was the entire industry he'd devoted his life to. He had made it as a high-paid consultant, but the large contracts were a thing of the past. Companies were shifting away from developing their own complicated technology for services they could rent from the cloud.

When I began to mentor Vaughn, he had fallen from Yellow

Level, where the business had come to him, back down to Orange Level. At Orange Level you are a Worker, chasing the same jobs as everyone else. You have lost your personal brand and identity—the one that moves people to seek you out for what you uniquely offer.

Vaughn knew it was time to make a change and needed an answer, but how does a Steel Genius shift to Green Performer if he is not naturally the strongest at coming up with innovative new business ideas? Not by trying to be a Dynamo Genius like me, but by following the same three steps in his own natural way.

Step One: Establish Your Enterprise

- *Do not* get caught up in your need for things to be perfect before you begin. And don't try to control all aspects of your business, holding on to the old and preventing growth.
- *Do* seek out business models that resonate with you that are generating the revenues and market flow that allow you to add value through your eye for detail and ability to analyze and systematize.

When I took Vaughn through his Future Vision and gave him a chance to consider what his future self would look like, what excited him most was the new wave in mobile payments. Until he focused in this way, he had seen the mobile payment wave as a threat to the expertise he had built. It made him fearful instead of excited. The idea that he could actually be a leader in this new wave was a new one and transformed his energy.

Vaughn created the picture of the ideal company he wanted to be a part of: a leader in the new mobile payment field. He "established his enterprise," and then instead of just starting it himself, he thought of how to position himself to be an ideal fit for such a business. He didn't want to be the one leading the company; he wanted to be the technology and operations expert inside it.

Vaughn set himself up as a "Leading Learner" in mobile payments. There was a time in the past when everyone was looking for a "Teaching Teacher"—someone who was an expert in the field with knowledge to share. Today, a Teaching Teacher is no longer good enough. Relying on past knowledge makes you out of date and out of touch. Everyone is now looking for Leading Learners, who are at the leading edge of their fields.

He set up social media accounts and started a blog on the latest news on mobile payments. He set up an email newsletter that he shared with those who were interested. Momentum grew, and people in the field who found Vaughn's newsletter and blog interesting passed it on to others.

It took less than six weeks of this new identity, sharing what he was learning, before Black Label Solutions, a leader in the new mobile payments systems that retailers were looking for in Australia, approached him. They found Vaughn's knowledge interesting and wanted him to work for them on their new mobile payment solution. The company matched Vaughn's ideal picture of the company he wanted to be a part of. He joined their team as their chief technology officer. Through this move he immediately found himself with his dream enterprise without needing to go through all the effort to set it up.

Step Two: Refine Your Rhythm

- *Do not* get stuck overanalyzing, needing all the answers before acting, or making judgments alone rather than as part of a high-performing team.
- *Do* use your eye for detail to set a schedule that you and your team can follow with a rhythm to grow the business in which each person is empowered in his or her role while you maintain control of the measures.

Vaughn had started with a rhythm of his own blogs and newsletter, but once he took on the role as CTO, he supported his Dynamo Genius CEO by setting the rhythm, measures, and metrics that allowed the business to grow effectively. Vaughn set policies and processes for the different areas of the business.

By setting himself up as a Leading Learner and maintaining that as a CTO, he stayed up-to-date with all the cutting-edge business models that the mobile payment companies were using in the United States and Europe. That way, he did not have to work things out from scratch but could draw on best practices that already existed in the new industry. The company went on to win a big contract to provide its mobile payment solution to the retail clients of one of Australia's leading banks. This led to a rapid growth path where reliable delivery is key and Steel Geniuses excel.

Step Three: Synchronize Your Steps

- *Do not* become too internally focused, where you are spending all your time reviewing your own measures and performance.
- *Do* leverage your time to look externally and connect the flow of your business to the flow of the market.

Steel Geniuses are often the best at securing financing, as they can present numbers and details credibly to potential financiers. This was perfect for Vaughn: His final step out of Yellow Level, and the next step for Black Label Solutions, was raising the money to continue with the firm's rapid growth.

Vaughn took the lead role on the financing, but mobile payments and raising capital for high-tech start-ups were both in their infancy in Australia. The angel investment and venture capital industry was in its winter season—not the best time to plant seeds! He looked to overseas markets for funding. He connected with investors in Europe and the United States who were already investing in the mobile payment market, where the industry was in its spring season. This led to an increase in the profile of both the company as well as Vaughn's standing in the industry on the global stage.

As Vaughn learned, improvements in communication and collaboration make it easier to start a global business than a local business today. You don't need to be stuck in the season of your local market. There is someone, somewhere in the world, that you can learn from and earn with who is in the season that suits your business and your genius.

Vaughn now has big prospects in a fast-growing industry, working in an entrepreneurial team without having to start his own business. He did it all by switching his focus from what opportunities he should chase to setting himself up with an attractive identity he was passionate about, so opportunities would chase him.

The Dynamo Path From Yellow to Green

Matt Riemann runs a successful physiotherapy, massage, and fitness business, Body Elite Management. He was always busy with clients and had spent years trying to work "on his business" instead of "in his business." Nothing had worked. Everyone came to his clinic to see him, and he hadn't been able to find the time to step out of the day-to-day work for some Superman Time without sales taking a big drop.

How could he move from Yellow to Green? How do you change the wheels on a moving bus? I began mentoring Matt, and together we listed his three biggest obstacles:

1. The clinic needed him to be working all hours to pay the bills, so he didn't have the time to be thinking strategically.
2. The clients all wanted him, so even though he had multiple physiotherapists and massage therapists, he was always busier than they were.
3. His team wasn't experienced at management, so he was unsure how much he could rely on them to take on more or whether he should bring in a general manager.

Everyone—from your customers to your team and partners— falls into the habits and expectations you set for them. By following the three steps out of Yellow, Matt transformed his business. In less than twelve months, he was able to spend most of his time away from the company, while the business became far more profitable.

Step One: Establish Your Enterprise

- *Do not* stay trapped in a space where everything relies on you and where you are always the first to act to drive things forward at your pace, leaving everyone behind.
- *Do* change the focus from you to the enterprise, where your enterprise has a stronger brand and more attraction than you do and your team is empowered to act and move things forward without you.

We started with Matt's Future Vision and the life he wanted to live. He wanted multiple businesses, more time for adventure, and to be a leader in cutting-edge health and wellness at the global level. We then set his company's unique niche: a leader in sports fitness. His biggest clients, we found, were sports teams that sent all their players to him. By knowing his niche, how could he focus his marketing toward sports teams? How could he package his products so he was the number one choice for *all* sports teams in the region? We set Matt's personal targets of how much time he would be serving clients (two days a week) and the financial targets for the company.

Next, we created a Green Level model for the company in which Matt would charge a much higher rate for his own time than that of his assistant therapists. That way he could be earning more in less time *and* set a career path for his therapists in which they could see that they could earn as much as Matt once they stepped up to his level. His therapists immediately became far more motivated—they could see how to earn more by increasing their skill levels and client base. They now had an incentive to work Matt out of his role, not leave him for another business.

Matt's biggest worry had been what his clients would think about paying more for his time. When he announced the new fee structure, he was surprised to hear many of them say, "It's about time." *If you're already too busy with too many clients, your clients already know you're charging too little.* Within three months, Matt was working with clients two days a week, and the company had higher revenues and profits than ever before.

The extra time also helped Matt address the problem of therapists being trained and leaving by turning it into an opportunity: He set up a massage school and physiotherapy academy, providing on-the-job career training for new therapists with a trainee charge for clients. This gave him a flow of new therapists that also became a profit center instead of a cost. Even if all the therapists left, he would still be making a profit and not need to go back to working five days a week.

As it turned out, with this new career path in his clinic, the therapists wanted a permanent position after training, and he got to choose from the ones who performed best.

Step Two: Refine Your Rhythm

- *Do not* keep coming up with new ideas to innovate your way forward, implementing these ideas as soon as you think of them and changing things on the fly.
- *Do* work with your team, especially your Tempo and Steel Geniuses, to set a rhythm that everyone can follow. Be sure everyone knows when you are reviewing and renewing strategy, roles, promotions, milestones, measures, and daily performance.

Now that Matt had a team, he had the time to put his creativity to work to solve his remaining problems one by one and work on the strategy of the business. Within six months, Matt had set up a loyalty program, designed new customer service processes, and created a vision and culture for the team. With new strategies in place, it was time to empower the team, beginning with a team meeting to share his vision.

Matt had never shared his strategy on the business with his team before. What would they think? As with all steps from one level to the next, our biggest anxieties come when we are unsure if the people around us will support us in moving up a level. *What if people won't pay extra to see me? What if my team thinks I'm just trying to do less work? What if they think I'm taking my business too seriously?*

As you might have guessed, the first meeting, in Matt's words, "Didn't go well." He tried to explain the company strategy, got blank looks, and halfway through changed the purpose of the meeting into a friendly get-together.

That's when we had a long talk about the power of *why*. Matt needed to share his dream for the company and attract team members to the dream: He needed to capture *why* he wanted to share leadership with them and what that meant in terms of extra responsibility. Matt called the team together again a few weeks later and asked who was up for playing a bigger game. He was surprised to find many on the team inspired by his vision and ready to step up. Over the next three months, the *team* put a rhythm in place that allowed them to monitor their roles and the performance of the company.

Matt visited Bali with his entire team recently after their most successful year ever. We noted how he had upgraded one of the perks of Yellow Level (running your own business and whisking yourself away to paradise to celebrate) to the similar perk at Green

Level (having your team run your business and whisking them *all* away to paradise to celebrate).

Step Three: Synchronize Your Steps

- *Do not* become too internally focused, spending all your time reviewing your own measures and performance.
- *Do* leverage your time to look externally and connect the flow of your business to the flow of the market.

The third step at every level turns on the flow. To get to Yellow Level, you monetized your moment, predicted your cash flow through a promotion, and then tested and measured your way to success. At Green Level, synchronizing your steps is about timing your promotions for maximum effect.

With the time that Matt now had to look externally, he found himself getting more excited about the pioneering work taking place in future medicine and personalized health. Because his business was now able to sustain itself profitably at Green Level, within a year of being stuck there, Matt now had the time and money to pursue a new venture, which is what Dynamo Geniuses love to do. He connected with pioneers in the latest medical technology and personalized medicine spaces, became a known entity at important international conferences, including presenting at Future Med in Silicon Valley, and has since been invited to speak to the UN and advise the US military on personalized health. He is now working on a groundbreaking mobile DNA and body-type analyzer with leading industry experts, fully in his flow and pursuing his life mission of a pain-free world.

Three Ways to Play From Yellow to Green

As is frequently the case with people trying to move out of Yellow Level, the biggest questions I got from the people I just discussed involved cost: *How do you manage the cost of a promotion if the biggest cost is people? How can you find the right people at the right level to manage your company?*

The answer is that there are three ways you can work with people, depending on the way you set up your partnerships and agreements.

Remember the Wealth Equation we discussed in the last chapter:

Wealth = Value × Leverage

When you build your partnerships, they will fit into one of these three variables in the equation. How you set your agreements up creates a different challenge you need to overcome.

COST-BASED PEOPLE

Having cost-based people means you hire them and have to pay them. This is the traditional way we think about employment. In the equation, a cost-based person is someone who you think will add Value to the team, but that means you need to add the Leverage and work out how to make the extra money to pay for them. *When you are getting started at Yellow Level, you want to minimize the cost-based people in your promotions.* Usually, cost-based people are in the Foundation Prism, expecting wages or payment for a contract based on delivering Value through an activity or deliverable. You, however, need to run faster to make the money by leveraging that Value.

REVENUE-BASED PEOPLE

Having revenue-based people means you partner with a person or company that is likely already at Yellow or Green Level. They are willing to work on a promotion in return for a share of the revenues. They know how to Leverage your Value and don't cost you anything unless they or the promotion have delivered the sales. All marketing and affiliate partnerships work this way. Most distributors and retailers and all "sale or return" partnerships work this way. Scott had revenue-based people as sales and marketing partners, and Renate had them as real estate agents. This allowed them to grow without adding to overhead. The challenge is that you need to make sure you are building the Value they can Leverage. That means improving your brand or product so the best players in the market would rather partner with you than anyone else.

PROFIT-BASED PEOPLE

As you move up the Wealth Spectrum, you look for profit-based people to join your team. These are people who know how to run a profitable promotion, hire the right team, and reach revenue targets. These are leaders who have had experience in both adding Value and Leveraging that Value. The problem is, most of these people are either running their own businesses already or are Green Performers working in companies that pay them more than you can afford. Using the Wealth Equation, the way to attract and keep profit-based people is by building your Wealth as they build the Value and Leverage.

Remember, *wealth isn't how much money you have; wealth is what you're left with if you lose all your money.* Wealth is your track record, connections, momentum, access to resources, and personal brand in the market.

This is the reason that moving up the Wealth Lighthouse is so important. You need to earn the right before you can attract the people you want at the right level. Orange Level Workers haven't yet earned the right to attract revenue-based players and profit-based performers. Yellow Level Players have earned the right to attract other revenue-based players but not profit-based performers. Green Level Performers have earned the right to attract the best revenue-based players and cost-based workers to work with, and Blue Level Conductors have earned the right to attract profit-based performers to manage the healthy flow of their investments and enterprises for them.

This is the key to ongoing financial freedom. You need multiple teams to manage multiple streams.

How about you? Are you currently working as a cost-based person? Or have you upgraded yourself to revenue-based with promotions where you are sharing in the risk and the reward with other partners? Or are you already capable of operating as a profit-based person where you can offer your Value to a Green Performer or Blue Conductor to generate profit for them and share in the reward?

Whoever you are, be sure you remember your path and are in a business that works for your genius. *Each of the four geniuses has a different path out of Yellow Level, but they also have a different type of business that they find greatest success in.*

The Four Types of Business

Too many people end up stuck and unhappy in Yellow Level or failing in a business completely because they blindly followed a formula that worked for someone else but will not work naturally for them. All businesses and investments fall into one of four different types: product-based, market-based, location-based, and transaction-based. These create an ecosystem within an industry, and as the seasons of that industry change, the power moves from one type of business to another.

While you can be a great leader in any type of business, each of these businesses is best suited to one of the four geniuses. To understand what I mean, consider my own industry: the personal and professional development industry, starting with my own genius.

Dynamo Businesses Are Product-Based

In the "spring season" of any industry, it is the people and companies with new and innovative products that are in the driver's seat. For these businesses, the key metrics are based on how many products they intend to sell and how much people will be buying the products for. At the beginning of the personal development industry, it was those with the content—first Napoleon Hill and Dale Carnegie and later Tony Robbins and Stephen Covey—who commanded the highest fees and led the market. These are all Dynamo Geniuses running product-based businesses.

Dynamo Geniuses come alive when leading start-ups and in creative, fast-changing enterprises. When in a product-based business, they *really* shine. When they partner up with market-based businesses and outsource to the other two types of business (see below), their business grows even more rapidly as they have the right infrastructure in place to support their growth.

Blaze Businesses Are Market-Based

In the summer season of an industry, the point of power moves from product-based businesses to market-based businesses. When there is so much choice of products out there, people would prefer to gather around like-minded people in communities where they can hear about the latest and best products. Thus, a market-based business is one whose key metrics are not based on how many products you sell, but on how many customers you have and the lifetime value of all the products and services you provide to each. As the personal and professional development industry moved to summer season, it was the entrepreneur networks and event organizers who could take their pick of the content creators.

Blaze Geniuses thrive in summer, as they are always at their best with their team and connecting to customers. They want to know what their customers want; then they seek out the product-based business partners that can provide it. They also look for the right location-based businesses to align themselves with, so they can change venues when they need to and when the crowds get bigger.

If you are a Blaze Genius, you can be of great value to any business when connecting to and leading people. But when you lead your own market-based business—in which you are focused on how to build the lifetime value for and monthly revenues from each customer—that's when you'll shine brightest.

Tempo Businesses Are Location-Based

In the autumn season of an industry, the wave moves from market-based businesses to location-based businesses. This is when there are many communities consuming many products, and they all seek a home. There are enough market-based businesses to support a location, be it a marketplace, shopping mall, or, in the case of the personal development industry, hotel venues and conference halls. A location-based business is one whose key metrics are not how many customers you have, but what capacity of your location assets you are utilizing. In the hotel industry, this is your occupancy rate. In the retail industry, this is your yield per square meter or square feet. The more market-based businesses you can attract, the more you can increase your capacity. The people who have the best venues make the money.

When I saw the personal and professional development industry move into autumn, we set up our Bali resort to be a venue for entrepreneurship and leadership development. We attracted other event organizers and could bring down the cost of our own events, as we owned the resort. Now we are planning to open more entrepreneur resorts around the world to support entrepreneurs setting up global businesses so they can work from anywhere and learn from everywhere.

Tempo Geniuses like Renate are perfect here as they are at their best when they are in constant activity, using their sensory awareness to serve. Whether that is in a restaurant, hospital, or stock market trading floor, Tempo Geniuses get in their flow when they are on location. If you are a Tempo Genius, you keep your team grounded regardless of the industry, but when you are in the center of a location-based environment, you really shine.

Steel Businesses Are Transaction-Based

In the winter of an industry, the wave moves from location-based businesses to transaction-based businesses. This is when everyone is in the market. They know the products, they have their communities, they have their meeting places, and everyone is looking for efficiencies and lower prices. This is when the wave moves to transaction-based businesses that have created systems to increase efficiencies, increase speed, and reduce costs. Transaction-based businesses, whether delivery companies like UPS or online firms such as Google, make their money by taking a percentage of every transaction. Their key metrics are the number of transactions and the amount they make on each regardless of the products, companies, or locations they are connecting.

The personal and professional development industry is moving into the winter, as customers know they can access any message directly from a blog, YouTube, a book, or a podcast. Everyone is looking for smarter, simpler ways to access the advice they need when they need it. This book and our online learning platform, GeniusU, are serving this shift and the need we all have today to clear through all the information to get to the direction.

If you are a Steel Genius, you can add value to any team through your attention to detail. But when you step into a transaction-based business, you reach your success fastest.

Finally, Remember: Spirit Organizations Are Contribution-Based

While all four geniuses have a natural way to create wealth most effectively, as you raise your spirit and wealth and grow your ability to create wealth, you grow your ability to contribute wealth.

All of us have the power to begin contributing today.

John D. Rockefeller began by giving 10 percent of the money he made as he earned it and continued growing that habit until he devoted his life to philanthropy. But you don't need to be a Rockefeller to automatically give some of what you get and create a river with a purposeful downstream. Remember: The more you contribute to that stream, the more you attract in return.

CHAPTER SIX SUMMARY

- Yellow Level is the first Enterprise Prism level, where everything relies on you.
- Yellow Level gives you freedom to be self-employed, but you need to keep showing up to keep the money flowing. At Green Level you have businesses that can work without you.
- You can move out of Yellow by following these three steps:

  Establish Your Enterprise
  Refine Your Rhythm
  Synchronize Your Steps

- Geniuses have a different strategy for these three steps that allows them to use their genius with a team of geniuses to support them.

- There are three excuses that stop us from moving from Yellow to Green: *I can't find people who can do it like me*, *I can't afford good people*, and *I'm too busy to find and train the right people*.
- You can spend your life at Yellow Level and keep your time freedom, but when you choose to move up, you master managing teams and types of people (cost-based, revenue-based, and profit-based) and eventually create multiple streams.
- There are four different types of business that suit the four geniuses: product-based, market-based, location-based, and transaction-based. All industries include all four types of business that rise and fall with the season of the industry.

Preflight Checklist: Green Level

Are you ready to move from Yellow to Green Level and reclaim your time? As with the other levels, your personal page on www.millionairemasterplan .com has assessments and Playbooks for each of the checklist points below. The exercise I have included here is adapted from the Playbook and covers how to refine the rhythm of your business to suit the five genius frequencies. You can find the complete version online.

Complete the checklist now: Tick yes or no. How do you rate? Then get to work on shifting each no to a yes.

Establish Your Enterprise

1. We have a compelling and unique Enterprise Promise that creates attraction of customers and resources.　　☐ Yes　☐ No

2. We have a business model that affords a leadership team and a Team Charter with a clear Flight Path for the team.　　☐ Yes　☐ No

3. I have selected and empowered a leadership team to lead the company with clear milestones and financial targets.　　☐ Yes　☐ No

Refine Your Rhythm

1. We have an annual rhythm of review and renew for
   our plan, promotions, projects, and processes.   ☐ Yes   ☐ No

2. I have a rhythm that keeps me in flow while the team
   has a weekly and daily rhythm that keeps each
   member in flow.   ☐ Yes   ☐ No

3. We have a Flight Deck with all measures and milestones,
   and we have a system to keep us on our Flight Path.   ☐ Yes   ☐ No

Synchronize Your Steps

1. We have an understanding of our profiles and
   strengths and have fit our positions to our profiles
   to stay in flow.   ☐ Yes   ☐ No

2. We are aware of the stage of enterprise we are in,
   and we are keeping to a frequency of action that
   suits the stage.   ☐ Yes   ☐ No

3. We are aware of the stages of our industry and are
   managing our expectations and promotions
   based on the season.   ☐ Yes   ☐ No

ACTION POINT

Refining Your Rhythm to Suit Your Genius

People at Yellow Level often take pride in their freedom to do what they want when they want. That's why most Yellow Level Players cannot build an enterprise without it growing into chaos. Your enterprise only gets into flow through a rhythm of manage and measure, review and renew.

When do you meet each week to review your key metrics? When do you meet every month to review your financials? How do you connect every quarter to review your team and projects and every year to renew your strategy?

Yellow Level Players often change strategy far too often while they fail to review key metrics often enough to keep the heartbeat of the enterprise in rhythm.

When you think of each of the five geniuses as elements and each of the elements as five frequencies, you can create a rhythm where your entire business can get into flow.

Enterprise Promise—The *Why?*

Your Enterprise Promise is your true north: Every action and every plan in the business points toward it. All frequencies have a time at which to renew and a time at which to review.

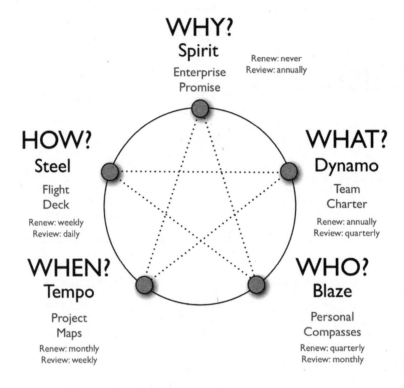

WHY?
Spirit
Enterprise
Promise

Renew: never
Review: annually

HOW?
Steel

Flight
Deck
Renew: weekly
Review: daily

WHAT?
Dynamo

Team
Charter
Renew: annually
Review: quarterly

WHEN?
Tempo

Project
Maps
Renew: monthly
Review: weekly

WHO?
Blaze

Personal
Compasses
Renew: quarterly
Review: monthly

The Enterprise Promise is never renewed, and it is reviewed annually.

What is your Enterprise Promise in one sentence? How well have you been fulfilling this promise? How will you fulfill it in the year ahead? Set a time to answer these questions and review the promise annually when you bring everyone together to align to your mission. (I run weeklong annual retreats for the leadership of my companies to review and get realigned around our Enterprise Promise.) Don't make sudden changes that others cannot follow midway through the year; hold off those big strategic decisions until your annual review. Your Enterprise Promise is like your company's DNA. So if you come up with a different Enterprise Promise, it's better to start an entirely new business with a new DNA.

Team Charter—The *What?*

Many companies have five-year plans or annual plans that no one looks at. The truth is, the world is changing much faster than it used to, and the people who can most easily keep the business on course are the ones on the front line. By giving everyone a chance to check in every three months on *what* is being achieved to fulfill your *why*, everyone has a chance to course-correct for the coming quarter. Checking in less frequently and changing direction more often both lead to the wrong frequency, out of tune with the rhythm of the team.

> *Your Team Charter is renewed annually and reviewed quarterly.*

What is your Team Charter for the coming year? Set a plan with your team for *what* will be achieved before deciding on *who* will do it. Once you have set your plan at the annual retreat, set quarterly reviews where the team meets for a day at the end of every quarter to review how you are doing against plan.

Personal Compass—The *Who?*

Someone owns each promotion and every process in a company. That means everyone on the team has both milestones and measures they are responsible for. The Personal Compass we use is like a job description. But most job descriptions are not written by the people doing the job and are only checked when someone is hired instead of being used as a compass to keep them on track.

Have your staff members empower themselves with their own Personal Compass. Give them responsibility not for a task or a function, but for a promotion they can lead. (You will find a template for your Personal Compass in the Refine Your Rhythm Playbook.)

Your Personal Compass is renewed quarterly and reviewed monthly.

The members on our team have a Personal Compass that they write themselves based on their roles and responsibilities in the Team Charter. This is reviewed every month in a personal review session and renewed once every quarter at our quarterly team meetings. As team members look at how they are doing in their milestones and measures, they come up with their own solutions to keep themselves on track and keep playing their part in the team charter. If they think the milestones and measures in the Team Charter need to change, they can make changes with the team. This rhythm keeps everyone empowered and takes the pressure off you to be making all the decisions as the team grows.

Project and Process Maps—The *When?*

In chapter 5, I explained how all flow is the result of projects and processes: Projects expand or enhance flow, and processes maintain flow. Projects have milestones with a beginning and an end, and processes have measures and are ongoing. Each person on the team has ownership on a project (we turn all our projects into promotions) and ownership on one or more processes.

Your Project and Process Maps are renewed monthly and reviewed weekly.

In my businesses, I am always looking to automate or outsource our processes but keep an eye on the measures. That frees me up to focus on promotions that expand or enhance the flow of the enterprise. There is a simple map for each project and process that team members use to know what they are each responsible for. This is renewed every month at their personal review, and it is reviewed every week at the half-hour team meeting, which we call the team huddle.

Your Flight Deck—The *How?*

Every enterprise has a Flight Deck: a shared document that shows the key measures in your business and what each is every week compared to your targets.

> *Your Flight Deck is reviewed weekly and renewed daily (or in real time).*

I make sure I have access to my Flight Deck for each business from my mobile phone and tablet so I can see all the important measures for each business in real time. Each measure is monitored by the person responsible for it, and in the weekly meetings, each person reports on how he or she is doing, what he or she is doing to course-correct, and if he or she needs help. By having this, we can celebrate our successes each week based on our Flight Deck, and we can see how everything links all the way through the frequencies to the DNA of the enterprise. This is Green Level thinking.

With a system that can increase your bandwidth, what Green Level promotion can you set up to invite other performers to play with you? Instead of asking, *How do I make money?* think about asking, *How can I help other people make money?*

FROM GREEN TO BLUE: PERFORMER TO CONDUCTOR

Measure:	Profitable cash flow through enterprise teams
Emotions:	Rhythm; culture; measurement
Cost of staying here:	Politics; maintenance; freedom
Focus needed:	Authority and capital
How did I get here?	Interdependence; preparation; ambition
How do I move up?	Anchor Your Authority; Perfect Your Processes; Build Your Balance

Congratulations, you've made it halfway up the Wealth Lighthouse! Green may be the middle level, but it's not about how far you have to go now, it's about how far you have come. You can see Blue Level from here—the domain of millionaires.

A Green Performer is like a musician in an orchestra, playing one instrument as part of the symphony, and the ultimate level in the Enterprise Prism is right in front of you: the Blue Conductor. A conductor doesn't play any instrument, but holds the baton, sets the rhythm, and keeps everyone playing together.

While performers face the audience, the conductors have their backs to the audience and face the performers. What this means in terms of wealth and business is that Green Performers work as part of high-performing teams in an enterprise where everyone is doing one thing. The Blue Conductors leave the small details of each enterprise to those Performers and instead focus on the key financials, on agreements, and on building access to resources and the best people.

At Blue Level, leaders have a separate meeting each month to monitor their entire portfolio with their investment teams, separate from any meetings with their Green Performers. All Blue Level investors have an accountant and a lawyer within their advisory teams for their own personal wealth, separate from the companies or assets that they invest in. Simply put, the financial score sheet at Blue Level is different from all the levels that came before, even at Enterprise Level. At Yellow Level, we are most focused on our business's cash flow. At Green Level, the profit-and-loss statements become more important. By Blue Level, the most important score sheet is our balance sheet.

For a Dynamo Genius like me who struggles with financials— I'm happier with visuals than numbers—the easiest way I found to grasp these differences comes from this quote: *"Establish the triangle and the problem is two-thirds solved."*

Establish the Triangle

A GPS can determine where you are relative to a number of satellites and then work out your exact location down to the nearest meter. Why then are so many people still lost in life? There are two reasons.

The first reason is that while we have very clear maps of our physical world, there have been no maps of the metaphysical world. Ancient cultures had these maps, but they have gone largely ignored or forgotten in modern times. *The Millionaire Master Plan* addresses that issue by giving a GPS or metaphysical map that you can follow to move up in wealth.

The second reason is that most of us aren't using in our lives the technique that an actual GPS employs to keep track of us: a method called triangulation.

It was the father of triangles, Pythagoras (creator of the Pythagorean theorem), who said, "Establish the triangle and the problem is two-thirds solved." What he meant is that we address most problems from only two points, such as "us and them" or "then and now"—a straight line connecting two points. When we add a third point, however, we get a triangle. Each point can now be seen in context with two other points. This gives us both detachment and perspective in every situation.

When you create your Future Vision, you create a triangle connecting your past, present, and future; you created a third point where you could step outside your journey and see your present life, your future life, and the path that connected one to the other. All the case studies from Yellow to Green in the last chapter featured people who created triangles to solve their problems. For example, when Scott created a set of criteria that his property clients would be happy to invest with, he created a triangle among his customers, his suppliers, and the criteria for them to do business together. When Vaughn created the criteria for the company he wanted to work with, he created a triangle among himself, the company he was seeking, and the criteria for a profitable partnership.

When we create that third point, we create a dynamic set of relationships that allow flow to happen. This is the relationship among the three steps at each level of the Wealth Lighthouse and among the three levels within each of the three prisms. That is also how every successful wealth creator works.

The power of triangulation may be ancient, but it is the foundation of modern-day accounting. The system, documented by

Luca Pacioli—who managed the wealth of the Medici family as they funded large parts of the Renaissance—is called double-entry accounting. It looks at all accounts as a triangle divided into a cash flow statement, a profit-and-loss (P&L) statement, and a balance sheet. Whenever you change a number in one statement, there is an equal and opposite change in another statement. Every transaction gets recorded as both a debit and a credit, so the triangle is always balanced. Understanding this triangle is the key to building your wealth. (I have created a video to explain how the three relate to each other at www.millionairemasterplan.com.)

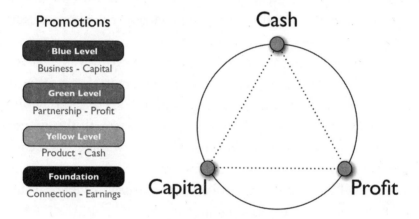

Whether you are looking for cash, profit, or capital return, there is someone on another point of a triangle looking for something different and willing to trade with you. Establish the triangle, and the problem is two-thirds solved. In short, money is simply a promise (currently backed by our governments), and all wealth is created through the flow of promises:

- Your cash flow statement shows your promises paid.
- Your profit-and-loss shows your promises delivered.
- Your balance sheet shows your promises made.

When you agree to deliver value, you are making a promise. When you deliver that value, it shows up on your P&L as a promise delivered (revenue) and on your balance sheet as a promise made and owed (receivable). When the customer pays, it shows up on your cash flow statement as a promise paid (receipt) and comes off the receivables on your balance sheet as a promise made and paid. Depending on how you time the flow of promises, you establish far more control of the cash flow you need when you need it.

Once I understood this, my early struggles to manage my finances (when all I saw were numbers and dollars signs) began to ebb. I now saw financials as simply journals to track the flow of promises, and all banknotes are just promises (called promissory notes). That's when my wealth opened up.

For example, in my publishing company when I was at Yellow Level I needed cash flow, so I went to Green Level printing companies that were looking for extra profit. I found one that was willing to give me six months' credit in return for me paying them 5 percent above market rate for their printing. I saved the extra cash, and they made extra profit. I then went to the more pioneering Green Level advertisers and offered a 50 percent discount if they paid for six months' advertising up front.

I got the cash, and they got double the value for their money. Raising money from the market this way was much easier than trying to get bank financing. My customers and suppliers were taking a risk with me and, by doing so, giving me their vote of confidence that I was delivering something they valued.

When my publishing business grew to Green Level and I looked for venture capital funding to grow, I had to prove I could provide what Blue Conductors seek: businesses and assets they can invest in that are likely to deliver a reliable return on investment.

When I reached Blue Level, my focus changed from tracking profits from businesses to tracking returns on my investments. This resulted in investment decisions each year that led to our personal monthly cash flow rising through the rest of the Ten Steps to a Million Dollars. My mentor was right. The higher you go, the easier it gets.

Blue Conductors trade cash for a return on investment. Green Performers trade returns in profit and capital in return for cash with Blue Conductors and trade cash in return for more profit with Yellow Players. These three form the triangle of the Enterprise Prism. We can all make these trades for free and only need to manage time (which we have a flow of) and trust (which we can grow with care) in order to build our track record of delivering on the promises behind those trades. Keep this in mind as we prepare to ascend the three steps from Green Level to Blue Level.

The Three Steps From Green to Blue

Everyone has the opportunity to get to Blue Level. You don't have to be super-intelligent, unreasonably hardworking, or freakishly talented, either. In fact, you will find many Blue Conductors to be remarkably normal; they even downplay any special skills they might have, deferring instead to their Green Performers.

In addition to an understanding of the wealth triangle, what people at Blue Level all have in common is that they earned the respect and loyalty of their teams, partners, and financiers by being dependable and consistent in the authority they are building in their markets. That is what informs the three steps from Green to Blue and the genius paths through these steps:

1. **Anchor Your Authority:** Blue Conductors attract Green Performers by being seen as leaders and influencers in their industries. They have proven that they can marshal the resources needed to make things happen. Like the coach of a sports team, they don't need to be on the field playing. They are setting the strategy for the game.

2. **Perfect Your Processes:** Blue Conductors have taken their Green Level rhythms to new heights with a level of care and discipline that allows everything to stay in flow—both the flow of cash and resources *and* the flow of information— so they invest their time in the most important decisions while leaving the day-to-day to others. This means they have time to observe the movement of capital, talent, and resources across their enterprises.

3. **Build Your Balance:** Blue Conductors are most focused at their balance sheets and look at everything as an asset or a liability. This means both your financial balance sheets and your personal balance sheets—so that when things are going well you always consider the potential downside, and when things are going badly you always see the upside.

Before we proceed through these paths, consider these three statements of wealth in terms of your health.

The cash flow in your life and enterprise is like blood flow in your body. The purpose of the body is not to create blood, but without the blood flowing, the body will die. Yellow Players are focused on cash flow because without cash flowing, the game is over. For the body to grow, the rhythm of the lungs adds oxygen to the blood to grow your health. In the same way, profit in a business adds to the cash flow to grow your wealth. Green Performers are at a higher level of operation where they are adding profit to cash flow, allowing the business to grow.

When doctors know your lungs are working, your heart is pumping, and your vital signs are strong, they can focus on the health of your individual organs. The key to that health is not growing oversized organs but ensuring that all your organs are operating in balance.

Blue Conductors do the same thing in business by following these three steps and focusing on assets that add and contribute to the whole. A successful Blue Conductor is not seeking growth for growth's sake, but seeking balance between risk and reward, between cash flow and capital growth, and between expanding and enhancing.

The Tempo Genius Path From Green to Blue

When I was twenty-two, I met my first Millionaire Mentor, Michael Braunstein, who taught me the Ten Steps to a Million Dollars we covered in Red Level. Michael was a property investor in Columbus, Ohio, and a Tempo Genius who made his money investing in, building, and managing property developments. I worked with Michael in his string of apartment communities in return for mentoring, and in my first week I spent time assisting his Riverside Apartment complex manager, Melissa.

I joined Melissa when the complex was going through an upgrade and rents on the one hundred apartments were being increased by 40 percent as a result. Melissa was speaking to all the tenants in the community about the increase. Even though the upgrades completely justified the increases and would make life better, many had decided to leave and rent elsewhere, many of them choosing to move to a more affordable community down the road: Shannon Way.

Melissa was frustrated. "We have had many of these tenants for years," she said. "It's a shame to see them leaving now. We are making profit so we don't need to charge more. I hope Michael knows what he is doing." Melissa looked at the situation as a Green Performer: They had been reaching their profit targets. So why change what was already working?

After the first week I caught up with Michael and asked him straight out, "Why are you charging more money if you're already making money? Is it because the banks are charging you more? Or do you just want to make more profit?"

Michael took out a piece of paper and drew his different properties and the profit each was making. He then wrote next to each a much bigger number. "This," he said, pointing to the bigger number, "is the amount the banks are willing to value each of my properties at. When I increase the money I make in rental from a property, the bank is willing to increase the value of the property. If I make an extra $100,000 in rental from a property, the bank could be willing to value the property at ten times that, which means the value of the property goes up by $1 million.

"I'm in the middle of acquiring a new property and so when I sat with my investment team and bankers, and looked at all our different properties, Riverside was the development they were willing to revalue based on me increasing the rentals to bring in a higher return. As long as we reach a percentage of occupancy, which proves we can rent them at a higher amount, they are willing to revalue the property and give me the financing I need for my new development."

This was my first introduction to how you look at life very differently at Blue Level where everything multiplies. Earnings to one person can simply mean more profit, but it can mean ten times that amount—or more—when measured in capital value and return on investment. A $100 increase in profit in a retail store can multiply quickly if it is rolled out over a chain of fifty stores and then is translated into an increase in the share price and the value of the business when the business is valued as a multiple of profits.

When I asked Michael if he was bothered that he was losing customers to other developments, he said, "That's why I make sure I have a balanced portfolio."

I didn't know what he meant, so I said, "No, I mean really. You're losing customers. Many of the people who are leaving Riverside are going to another apartment community down the road."

Speaking in words I could understand then, Michael replied, "I know. I own Shannon Way as well."

So what were the steps that Michael and his Tempo Genius took to understand this in moving to Blue Level?

Step One: Anchor Your Authority

- *Do not* remain entrenched in your business as a key part of management, staying involved with day-to-day operations and thinking your eye for detail is necessary to keep things in balance.
- *Do* appoint and empower a Green Performer to lead the business and remove yourself from the daily operations, using your genius to build capital value in your market niche to become an authority in your industry.

As a Tempo Genius, you may become an authority in the markets like Donald Trump (deal making), George Soros (trading), or Warren Buffett (investing). Your sensory nature gives you a strong sense of timing. All Tempo Geniuses are more interested in exchange than innovation and must take the time they need before acting. For this reason, they anchor their authority by being grounded and down-to-earth in their analysis and delivery. They need to build a trust team to oversee their investments—including an accountant to measure their promises and a lawyer to protect their promises.

At an early age, Michael learned from his mentor, one of the pioneers in US apartment communities, how to build a management team for each of his developments so he could invest his time in seeking funding and finding the right deals. He also had the time to focus on the right things for his genius in the business, which leads to step two.

Step Two: Perfect Your Processes

- *Do not* get caught up in judgment calls while overseeing your businesses.

- *Do* fine-tune the processes and policies of your businesses so there is a smooth flow of cash and resources, and the process for setting strategy, innovating, marketing, and upgrading systems and talent ensures that your businesses stay current.

Michael told me what was most important for Blue Conductors to keep an eye on within their businesses: "names and numbers"—the key people and metrics that drive 80 percent of your success. But when you are at Blue Conductor level, time becomes precious, and every moment counts. By having a process to keep you in the "right place at the right time," you open the space to keep an eye on the business and for luck to happen.

Tempo Geniuses like to be hands-on, so Michael set up a process to connect with his staff without interfering in management. When meeting with his general managers, he was most interested in the people who were making the biggest impact in the business (clients, staff, contractors, partners, and competitors) and the key measures on the Flight Deck. He set up a process with tours regularly around his properties, new properties in the area, and land auctions.

Step Three: Build Your Balance

- *Do not* remain focused on the transactions taking place within your business, seeking to maximize the quality of exchange through people and services.
- *Do* shift your focus to capital value, setting targets for your asset values and returns on investment.

Thinking back to the five myths we covered in going from Yellow to Green Level, the best property investors and Tempo Geniuses like Michael do not make their money by sitting back blindly enjoying passive income but by actively growing their portfolio and keeping an ear to the ground. Michael's success didn't come overnight—few Tempo Geniuses' successes do. It came from consistently focusing in the same field and growing his promotions from his first development with partners at Yellow Level (where he owned very little) to Green Level with a team, until eventually he had a number of different developments, each run as a separate company with a separate team as a Blue Conductor.

Michael had a small team overseeing all these businesses, with his accountant and lawyer keeping everything in order. He used his Tempo Genius strengths to plan each year a year in advance, knowing what assets he would be revaluing, getting a return on, selling, or buying. The shifts in his portfolio generated millions in cash flow each year, so he was never reliant on earned income for any cash.

The Steel Genius Path From Green to Blue

Chandresh Pala runs businesses in India and London. When I began mentoring him, we found he was a Steel Genius stuck at Infrared Level, using his cash to fund his businesses. He also had properties that he had bought, but they were in negative cash flow as well.

When I first began working with Chandresh, I asked him what he would choose for his future, if he could choose anything. "I'd like to be working as a Blue Conductor," he replied. "I'd love to be able to invest in tech start-ups and use my Steel Genius to add value to them."

So Chandresh took the Blue Level "fourth gear" path out of Infrared: We set a plan for him to reorganize his assets, pay down his debts, and limit the money he was putting in his business every month. He had a property vacant, waiting on higher rents, and we simply rented it at a lower rate so he would benefit from the cash flow and go cash positive.

Within three months, Chandresh had reorganized his personal finances and was cash flow positive. This hadn't been his initial focus when I met him, but taking a version of what became the Millionaire Master Plan Test had shocked him into taking action—and following the Steel path from Infrared to Yellow to Green and, finally, to Blue.

Step One: Anchor Your Authority

- *Do not* be internally focused, using your Steel Genius to keep fine-tuning the measures and systems of your business— that was the Steel winning formula at Green Level, but it's the losing formula at Blue Level.
- *Do* use your Steel Genius to become an expert and source of knowledge in your market niche, building the team to support you to connect with the influencers in the industry.

Chandresh had been funding his event technology company, Coconnex, and also had taken on the role of CEO. He switched that around by putting in a fixed amount as a loan for six months. Now, instead of going negative, he had a loan earning interest in his portfolio and a company with a six-month runway to turn to profit. He then put a Blaze Genius general manager in place, so he could free himself up to follow the steps he needed to be operating as a Green Performer (the same steps I took with Peter in my publishing company).

As Coconnex turned around and with more sales coming in, Chandresh rebranded one of his businesses, Cohezia, into a tech accelerator, welcoming applications from technology companies. Using his strength as a Steel Genius to easily increase efficiencies and improve systems in start-ups, he made this the unique feature in his accelerator, offering a range of services to start-ups that were looking for their second round of funding and support in growing their company.

To anchor his authority, Chandresh turned Coconnex into the first investee company of Cohezia—he made his own company his first customer. He then started connecting with the investment community by joining angel investor meetings.

That led to step two.

Step Two: Perfect Your Processes

- *Do not* get stuck managing and measuring the processes within your company, focusing on how to increase profitability.
- *Do* put the team in place to manage and measure these processes for you, so you can oversee the company from the outside and implement the processes that allow you to monitor the trends and opportunities to maximize the capital value of the business and your assets.

By seeing his own company as an investor, Chandresh's approach changed entirely, from coming in with his "Green Level hat" on (asking how he could generate more sales and make more profit) to coming in with his "Blue Level hat" on (asking whether he was getting a return on investment with his financing and whether his leadership teams were delivering value for money).

The result was that Chandresh could see his business with more clarity and less stress, with the right level of leadership—and trust in that leadership—to lead the company better than he could. This gave him even more time to connect with the angel investor community. Within six months Chandresh had been invited to be part of one of England's leading mentoring and investment networks, TIE. As a mentor in a network with thirteen thousand members across fourteen countries, Chandresh began attracting opportunities from both investors and investee companies.

Step Three: Build Your Balance

- *Do not* keep using the cash flow statement and profit-and-loss as your main scoreboards to judge your success—make them secondary to your balance sheet.

- *Do* establish a portfolio statement as your main scoreboard, giving you clear forecasts and actuals on your cash return on investments and yield on each asset and thus growing your access to capital.

Chandresh changed his outlook with a focus on his assets. By valuing his company, he saw how he could raise funding to match his own by putting in place a five-year plan and forecast for the company's growth. Making short-term wins in profitability was no longer as important as following a trend line in the plan so potential investors could see the company was delivering on expectations. That gave the five-year forecast more credibility, increasing Chandresh's ability to raise investments not only for Coconnex but also for Cohezia's investment fund.

Chandresh then hired a general manager for Cohezia who is now creating the template of processes and measures that can be used across all the companies they are investing in.

But Chandresh's story takes a cautionary turn here for everyone, especially for Steel Geniuses: Following the Millionaire Master Plan doesn't mean that the moment you begin using these steps everything will be clear sailing or that you can stop everything and think the boat stays on auto-pilot.

I met Chandresh recently and, while he was excited by his progress, he was back to being stressed and unclear about the future. He began asking me for advice on growing his business. I paused, as my mentor had many years earlier, and asked, "How are your personal finances?"

Chandresh had been so busy building his accelerator business that he had let his personal finances fall back into Infrared. We tracked back the few months that he had let this happen without noticing (he had simply gotten busy with other things and so had stopped measuring his money).

The good news is that within a week, Chandresh turned it around and got out of Infrared with a renewed focus and clarity. The speed with which he could turn things around came from understanding the GPS of the Millionaire Master Plan: triangulating his position at *every* level from Infrared through Blue. The map won't stop Chandresh or you from getting lost when you stop paying attention to it, but the faster you return to the map to check your position, the faster you can get yourself back on track.

The Dynamo Genius Path From Green to Blue

Richard Alderson is a Dynamo Genius who is passionate about making a difference in the world.

When I started mentoring Richard, he was primarily focused on co-founding UnLtd India. This group advises, supports, and provides funds to small social enterprises in India, using money raised from foundations and corporate donors. Prior to this, Richard spent time in the corporate world and subsequently at UnLtd, a network of social entrepreneurs in England.

The problem was that Richard only paid himself what he needed and put the rest into the growth of his business. His personal cash flow wasn't negative, but it wasn't positive, either. He was at Red Level. When I began mentoring Richard three years ago, and told him this was a problem and his first focus needed to be his own personal wealth, he couldn't understand why that was important. In fact, it felt like the opposite of what he believed in.

"It's not about the money," he said.

"If you are just getting by, then every decision you make is a money decision. So it's all about the money," I replied.

As long as Richard wasn't in a position to easily write a personal check for $10,000, it would always feel like $10,000 was a lot of money. If he couldn't write a personal check for $100,000, that would always feel like a lot of money. At Blue Level, writing checks for $100,000 is easy; the promotions that Blue Conductors focus on are all in the millions of dollars.

Richard needed to see that the language and thought process of someone who is used to writing checks in six figures and seven figures is very different from the language and thought process of someone who writes them in three figures or four figures. He needed to understand that his relationship with money at a personal flow level had a direct impact on the decisions he made about money in his job or business.

"You can't help the poor by being poor," I said. "Build your personal flow and use that as your steps up the lighthouse. Imagine how different your outlook would be if each week you wake up with another $20,000 in extra cash to put toward something. That's a million dollars extra a year in your pocket. What would you do with that money?"

Richard thought about it. "I'd invest it in social entrepreneurs," he said.

"Great! So stop thinking about helping social entrepreneurs with all your time and start thinking about investing in them with your money."

Now he needed to find his Dynamo Genius path to Blue Level.

Step One: Anchor Your Authority

- *Do not* be busy constantly starting up new ventures at Green Level, putting all your own cash from one business into the next.
- *Do* focus on an industry in which you want to anchor your authority and attract all the best performers and the smart money, so you can have others grow and start the businesses you are invested in using outside funding to leverage your genius.

I suggested Richard change his business model from raising money through donations to creating a social enterprise fund where investors would get a return. And instead of approaching people with money to invest as a client, he could approach them as equals looking to co-invest with them.

This would change not only the way Richard communicates with potential investors but also the way he views the social enterprises they were investing in. Richard began to connect to the main social entrepreneur networks and conferences around the world, and today he has built a reputation as a leading change maker supporting social entrepreneurs in India.

Step Two: Perfect Your Processes

- *Do not* keep making decisions based on your interpretation of the data, where everyone is still relying on your instincts and vision in deciding on what to invest time and money in (or not).
- *Do* build a team with a Steel Genius to create the metrics and measures for your businesses that everyone in the team can interpret and understand, so you empower others to assess the viability and suitability of the right investment deals and business deals you bring to them.

While Chandresh used his Steel Genius to add value to his investments through his analytical skills and systems thinking, Richard could use his Dynamo Genius to add value to his investments through his creativity and strategic thinking. I advised him to set up a process where he or a team member would sit on the board of each company they invested in and support each social entrepreneur.

In Richard's past model, his cash had not grown consistently— a common problem when you are buying or managing assets and not yet operating at Blue Level: Cash is dependent on capital, so cash flow is not consistent. It comes in big chunks when you sell a property or business and goes in equally big chunks when you buy the next. The result is that you end up asset rich and cash poor.

I showed Richard the process by which he could manage cash flow more effectively via three flows: an investment fee that gets paid when a new investment is made, a management fee that gets paid for the consultancy they provide, and a cash return from the dividends from each investment. All Blue Level Conductors perfect their processes so each area of value is rewarded with cash, making their business more sustainable through the ups and downs of the market.

Step Three: Build Your Balance

- *Do not* stay focused on revenues, profits, and the growth of your business.
- *Do* shift your focus and use your Dynamo Genius to be creative in how you are building your portfolio, managing resources, and raising capital.

Since Richard had multiple businesses, as soon as he moved to positive personal cash flow, he went from Red to Green Level. To move to Blue Level, however, required a change in his Dynamo Genius mind-set.

At a higher level in the lighthouse, you begin to see connections you cannot see when you're lower. This is when you truly ignite your genius, having a wider impact by taking a wider view.

Richard's second business, Journeys for Change, takes leaders on immersive journeys to help them make more impact in the world. His third business, Careershifters, helps mid-career professionals find more fulfilling work. His fourth, Impact DNA, helps people discover their unique path to making the most impact in the world—and is based on my Wealth Dynamics. By thinking at Blue Level, Richard began reorganizing how his businesses worked with each other by leveraging more effectively. Journeys for Change is highlighting the work of some of UnLtd India's investees, Careershifters has partnered with Journeys for Change to run journeys for people looking to shift into more meaningful work, and Journeys for Change is integrating Impact DNA into its learning curriculum.

The Blaze Genius Path From Green to Blue

Emma Ponsonby is a Blaze Genius living in Dubai. For many years she worked for a marketing consultancy, helping fashion labels in Europe and the United States set up their online stores. She had the idea of starting her own business in online retail, and she moved to Dubai to seek out retailers who would want a similar service.

I met Emma after she'd spent a year struggling to get her business started. She had her hands full running the business without paying herself, and her small team had yet to attract their first clients. They were targeting the main shopping malls but were still waiting for decisions from potential clients.

Once she found her Blaze Genius winning formula through these three steps, she climbed from Infrared to Green to Blue Level within a year.

Step One: Anchor Your Authority

- *Do not* remain focused on the leadership of the team and the connections with clients—your winning formula at Green Level is your losing formula when moving to Blue.
- *Do* build and establish a leadership team so you can invest your time connecting with Blue Level investors and enablers, establishing a higher level of authority with both the resources and the performers you need to grow.

When I began mentoring her, Emma created a Future Vision that looked very different from her original plan. Instead of chasing clients to build their online stores, Emma switched strategies to create her own global online fashion store. She set a one-year plan with the number of fashion labels and shoppers she would attract. Her team divided the plan into milestones and got focused on delivering on them while she went out to get financing.

Emma used her Blaze Genius to connect with the key figures and top brands in the industry. Without spending all her time in the office, she was more energized, and her team became more empowered. By spending time together with Blue Conductors who had questions on her business related to risk and reward, she learned the Blue Level language. With this change of focus and new understanding, she attracted them to her; within six months, she had raised funds for the business based on her plan valuing the business at more than $3 million.

Step Two: Perfect Your Processes

- *Do not* stay in the business and lead from the front, managing the rhythm of the company yourself.
- *Do* appoint a strong Steel Genius to manage your processes and policies and an accountant and a lawyer to support your deals and partnerships, giving you the freedom to travel and monitor the growth of your business and assets from a distance.

As a Blaze Genius, the bigger the game you play, the better the people you attract. Emma attracted a team of world-class professionals to support her. She attracted a group of advisers and kept to a process that kept her up-to-date with operations while attracting international interest.

Blaze Geniuses always do best at this when they have a strong

Steel Genius to manage their processes for them and ensure that the details and processes are in place when they meet those potential partners, team members, and investors. This is what Emma's new leadership did for her: To maintain cash flow through the fund-raising process, and to show proof of concept to potential investors and sponsors, the team launched a beta site while Emma was connecting with others.

Step Three: Build Your Balance

- *Do not* ignore the financials or the need to learn the language of investment, financing, risk, and return.
- *Do* use your Blaze Genius to surround yourself with a group of advisers and connections who speak the language of Blue Conductors, so you can build your balance sheet through their support.

Within her first year, Emma connected with celebrities, the heads of fashion brands, investors, sponsors, and major clients. With her Blaze Genius, she has also made connections among them through her, creating new opportunities within her network while growing her business.

This is the Blaze Geniuses' ultimate winning formula at any level: creating opportunities from their connections. But moving from Green to Blue Level, the next venture comes from those opportunities, because Blazes' businesses are operating through high-performing teams, not them.

A year after we began working together, Emma was radiant and transformed from the Infrared Level she had been at a year earlier. Her businesses had become a vehicle for her to grow personally and be of service—She let her businesses and assets take her to her highest potential instead of spending all her time serving her businesses.

Four Types of Investments

As you take these steps and follow your genius path to Blue Level, you will find that your genius becomes increasingly important in not just making but also keeping your wealth. *The undoing of many wealth creators is that they make their money through their winning formula only to lose it all with their losing formula.*

Here are the types of investments your genius should focus on—and the types to avoid—to stay in your flow.

Dynamo Investments Are Innovation-Based

The winning formula of Dynamo Geniuses is in seeing things that others can't. When they choose to invest in fast-growth companies, property developments, or businesses and properties that they can add value to through their innovation and development skills, and then resell or refinance, they build their portfolios most rapidly.

The losing formula for Dynamo Geniuses is their poor sense of timing. Dynamos are too often overoptimistic and over-ambitious when it comes to what to expect from the market. Avoid trying to outsmart the market through timing and negotiation or getting into riskier trading markets like options or futures. Even when riding a winning streak, Dynamos will find the money they make is lost when they overtrade or overextend themselves. If this is you, it's better to find one of the other Geniuses to manage some of your portfolio—your weaknesses are their strengths.

Blaze Investments Are Partnership-Based

The winning formula of Blaze Geniuses is in their ability to attract the right opportunities by being connected to the right people. When they choose to pursue investment partnerships with opportunities that deliver assets at a wholesale value or on terms that others simply cannot get, they excel. These can be business and property investments or partnerships in which they are funding a project or transaction that gives them predetermined returns.

The downside of Blaze Genius is in a limited attention to financial details: sitting with a spreadsheet and managing investments with an eye on tight margins, percentage returns, and yield management. Getting stuck with a property portfolio or trading system that requires constant monitoring will leave Blazes overwhelmed and undercapitalized. Blazes who have more cash than they know what to do with should hire a Steel Genius to manage investments like this while they stay in flow making deals and partnerships with others.

Tempo Investments Are Timing-Based

The winning formula for Tempo Geniuses is the losing formula of Dynamo Geniuses: using their ability to time the markets and to know when to buy and sell. That doesn't mean Tempos are going to be experts at this the moment they begin, but in the right environment, working with the right experts, the investments they excel at will be businesses, assets, and properties that they can trade.

The losing formula of Tempo Geniuses is the winning formula of Dynamo Geniuses: innovating their way to success. Tempos should steer clear of speculative investments where they need to add value or creativity to turn a low-value asset to a high-value asset. Keep away from new start-ups and investments that have no quick exit. Tempo Geniuses work best when they stay nimble and their investments are liquid.

Steel Investments Are System-Based

The winning formula for a Steel Genius is the Blaze Genius loser: paying attention to the details and reading the financials. It takes time to build all their skills, but by investing time in reading the numbers with their accountants, Steels will find smart ways to create ongoing cash flow by focusing on stable assets such as dividends from businesses or rental yields in properties.

The losing formula of Steel Geniuses is the winning formula for Blaze Geniuses: trying to be at the right place and right time in every conversation to catch the right opportunities. Steel Geniuses' success comes not from finding people but from finding what assets work for them and multiplying them. Steels don't need to do the wheeling and dealing in the marketplace. They are focused on the more stable and predictable investments and find returns for which Blazes don't have the patience.

And Remember: Spirit Investments Are Charity-Based

As you move up to Blue Level, you will find that you have also earned the right to give more than ever before. While we can all give to the causes we care about right now, as your flow grows, your power to give—and have that giving make an enormous impact—also grows.

As you take greater percentages of your flow and contribute it charitably, with no expectation of return, those donations become a driving force for moving you up the Wealth Lighthouse. This giving does wonders for others and gives you a greater purpose that adds meaning to your work and fulfillment to your life. If you move to Blue Level without this greater purpose, you will simply lose momentum: Personal success will no longer be a driver powerful enough to lift you up.

Only by turning our wealth from an opportunity to an obligation—where we see it as our duty to make more in order to give more—will we maintain momentum. That is why when we ask *Why?* with our spirit, our sense of purpose leads us to the highest levels.

CHAPTER SEVEN SUMMARY

- Green Level is the second enterprise level, the level of high-performing teams.
- At Green Level, you have businesses that can work without you. But moving up to Blue Level gives you the power to have multiple streams from multiple teams.
- You can move out of Green by following these three steps:

  Anchor Your Authority
  Perfect Your Processes
  Build Your Balance

- Geniuses have a different strategy for these three steps that allows them to shift to Blue Conductor Level.
- There are four different types of investments that suit the four geniuses: Dynamo investments that are innovation-based, Blaze investments that are partnership-based, Tempo investments that are timing-based, and Steel investments that are systems-based.
- As a Green Performer you master managing teams, which earns you the right to move to Blue Conductor, where you can attract many performers, all with their own teams and their own streams.

Preflight Checklist: Blue Level

Are you ready to move from Green to Blue Level—the land of the multi-millionaires and billionaires? As with the other levels, your personal page on www.millionairemasterplan.com has assessments and Playbooks for each of the checklist points below. The exercise I have adapted from the Playbook for this chapter is how to anchor your authority.

Complete the checklist now: Tick yes or no. How do you rate? Then get to work on shifting each from a no to a yes.

Anchor Your Authority

1. I have a cash-generating asset portfolio that is the anchor of my wealth and grows in line with my Flight Path.   ☐ Yes ☐ No

2. I have a trust structure and team that all my assets and enterprises flow to and are measured in.   ☐ Yes ☐ No

3. I am an established authority in my industry and attract high-level leaders to manage my assets and enterprises.   ☐ Yes ☐ No

Perfect Your Processes

1. All my assets and enterprises share the same process of review and renew, taking little of my own time.   ☐ Yes ☐ No

2. I have one common process and set of criteria for buying, holding, or selling my assets and enterprises.   ☐ Yes ☐ No

3. I have a system to assess new opportunities and talent, and to keep me at the right place, right time.   ☐ Yes ☐ No

Build Your Balance

1. I have a rhythm that enables me to maintain a balance of time across all areas of my portfolio and add value where needed most.   ☐ Yes ☐ No

2. I hold a long-term view of my industry and assets, and I have processes to keep me up-to-date with everything.   ☐ Yes ☐ No

3. I keep a balance among my life, portfolio, and roles at different levels of the spectrum to remain vital and versatile.   ☐ Yes ☐ No

ACTION POINT

Three Questions to Anchor Your Authority

You have seen the need to master teams so your teams can manage your streams. The challenge comes in finding the right performers to join you when you are still a Green Performer yourself.

Performers want to work with Conductors who can bring together the resources needed to work on million-dollar projects. You build these profitably from the moment you are running promotions at Yellow Level; by the time you are at Blue Level you have them all in place. The key to attracting performers is to prove to them that *they will play better music with you as the conductor than by playing without you.* This is what it means to anchor your authority. Three key things must be in place if you are to attract great performers:

1. An authority in your numbers: your portfolio
2. An authority in your leadership: your trust team
3. An authority in your resources: your network

Answer these three questions and complete the exercises as you take the steps to anchor your authority:

1. Do you have a cash-generating portfolio as the anchor for your wealth?

While you may own assets under your own personal name when you get started, by Blue Level you want to own your portfolio of assets under a trust or a holding company. The key to your portfolio is measuring your cash return on investment each year (net of the cost of any loans or liabilities) for each asset, whether it is a business, a property, the stock market, a bank account—any asset where your money is stored.

Set the right format to see all your assets in one portfolio (you will find a template for this in the Blue section of your personal page). Set your targets for each year in your cash return and capital growth before you decide about any specific assets. Then make the decisions you need to make with your team on how each asset needs to perform in the coming year so you reach your targets: Whether you increase the return of the asset, decrease the cost of liability, revalue, reallocate, buy, or sell.

Your ability to generate higher returns on your investments will have everything to do with how you use your natural genius and where you have your authority. What is the area in which you want to be an authority in your investments? Pick the area that suits your genius, and pick an industry that you are passionate about.

2. Do you have a trust team and team structure to grow your authority?

The right corporate and investment structure has everything to do with where you want to be investing and running your businesses. Set up the structure so it is suitable for your market, not for where you live. In other words, if you are growing a global business, don't set up your investment structure with your local lawyer and bank.

That is why you need to have a trust team of an accountant and a lawyer who can grow with you based on where you are going. Get one in place by sharing your path of where you are and where you are going. Share your portfolio and make them a part of your plan.

Now comes the part that moves you out of the Green Performer Level: Select, source, or attract a Performer to expand and enhance each of your assets so you aren't operationally involved in any of them. Factor into the return that there will be a cost for managing that asset. But better to receive half of the return on most assets with someone else managing them than for you to try to hold on to all of them and then lose your most precious asset: your time.

If you have been at Green Level for so long that you cannot imagine having someone else manage without you being involved, the easiest way to practice is to join another company as an adviser or board member at the strategic level. Believe me, you won't ask questions at the board meetings like, "Did you answer all your emails today?" You will immediately find yourself looking at the broader strategic issues that the company is facing; that will in turn give you a different perspective on your own business and time.

3. Are you attracting high-level leaders, resources, and opportunities?

Based on your industry, you will find that the Conductors who are managing the resources in the market are investing their time with trusted connections they have built over time. To find the right Conductors for you, answer these questions:

- Who are the top three conductors in your industry that you should connect to?
- Where are the top performers in your industry being attracted?
- Where are the major venues, events, and groups where resources are being exchanged?
- Where are the places where the inside opportunities are being shared?

The easiest way to build trust and connections with other Blue Conductors is to participate in their promotions (they are always running a promotion to launch, buy, or sell their next project, business, or investment)—and then run your own Blue Level promotion with their involvement or the involvement of people they trust.

Anchoring your authority takes time, but you have the cash flow at this level to fund your time. If you are ready to make it your mission to move to Blue Level, follow the rest of the online Playbooks to guide you there.

Chapter 8

FROM BLUE TO BEYOND: CONDUCTOR TO LEGEND

Measure:	Strong cash flow from million-dollar portfolio
Emotions:	Calm; patience; clarity
Cost of staying here:	Critics; isolation; loss of passion
Focus needed:	Trust and promise
How did I get here?	Risk management; asset management; detachment
How do I move up?	Trump Your Trust; Capitalize Your Currency; Connect Your Community

The most frightening experience I have ever had was on a trip to New Zealand. A friend took me to Nevis, which at the time had the highest bungee jump in the world. I remember standing on the platform, looking four hundred meters down to the rocks of the river below. The long rope tied to my ankles weighed against me. I was scared to death.

That's when the guide said to me, "Don't think of this like you're jumping. Think of it like simply letting go. Gravity will do the rest."

He was right. I had to let go of what I was holding on to in order to experience a new freedom. Yes, I was terrified, but if I let go, I would make a quantum leap in what I was willing to experience.

And so I did. And in return, I experienced what it felt like to fly.

Quantum Leaps Everywhere

When we started this journey, I told you about my first quantum leap in the way I was thinking the night my car was repossessed in Singapore, and I resolved to get out of Infrared and put in place the first steps of what became the Millionaire Master Plan. The rest of my climb did not require what I call my quantum leaps like the one that night or the one I had before I jumped off the bungee platform. Or did they?

The scientific definition of *quantum leap* is "one in which electrons jump from one quantum state to another." Do you remember in science class drawing atoms of different elements with rings of electrons? Each ring represented a different quantum state. Electrons jump from one ring to another when there is a change to the atom.

The most common example of this in the universe is the nuclear fusion in stars when two hydrogen atoms collide to form one helium atom. The result is that the two nuclei fuse into one, and an electron goes through a quantum leap, giving off a photon of light. Billions upon billions of these quantum leaps occur every moment, producing the light of our sun and the sparkle of stars in the night sky.

It's easy for us to think that quantum leaps happen only occasionally in life and forget that we are the result of quantum leaps and live in a world lit up by quantum leaps. Every day when I wake up, I remind myself that I am a part of this incredible world of light. Every day I have the choice to stay stuck in the same state, or I can take a quantum leap and be a part of the light. It's another day in the lighthouse.

You have seen how every level of the lighthouse requires a dramatic shift in the way we listen, think, and act. Each level forces us to look at things differently as our flow grows. Each level is like a radio station, connected on the dial to all the others but each at a different frequency. A simple shift of the dial, and the music we hear is entirely different.

Making it this far up the Wealth Lighthouse has also required letting go, just as I let go on the bungee jump platform. Sometimes it meant letting go of what you just learned weeks or months before to get you to the next level. If you were part of the majority of people in the world, you started in the Foundation Prism (at Infrared, Red, or Orange Level) and had to give up the freedom of choice or movement you earned there. You had to unlearn the steps that got you to one level to climb up to the next. Holding on to either freedom of choice or freedom of movement and what you attach your self-worth to at the previous level is how you get stuck at that level.

So you learned to let go, and in return you gained wealth, achieved so much success, and gave back more than you might have ever imagined. You are now among the minority of people in the world who have moved into the Enterprise Prism. And if you have moved through to Blue Level, you have earned the right to move beyond this stage, to the creation of the music itself: the third prism, the Alchemy Prism.

Blue Conductors have mastered the art of designing social leverage. We know how to create teams to manage our streams and are enjoying the freedom of movement this provides. We have little need for others to love our ideas, for working hard, or for interfering in the endeavors of our leaders. We attach our self-worth to the growth in our resources, which includes the high-level influencers we are now connected to.

When we reach Blue Level, the higher calling to be a Trustee for our industry or cause inevitably arrives. Now you need to decide whether you are willing to step up as a leader and role model for your industry or your cause. To move to Indigo Level and into the Alchemy Prism means letting go once more, specifically to the attachment you have to your freedom of movement, and to connect your self-worth to the legacy you will leave in your circle of impact.

The Alchemy Prism is where all the rules of the game are made. In the last hundred years, we have largely delegated how the rules of the game are made to large institutions and governments. This was not always the way things were.

In the days of the Renaissance, private families, scientists, artists, and architects made the rules. In the early days of America, the pioneers and entrepreneurs made the rules. In each case, they moved from being the Trustee of their movement to the Composer of the next. They rewrote the music when it went out of tune. Today, with the growth of the Internet and global economy, we are again seeing change makers and leaders choosing to step up and make the rules of the game on the global stage. Crowds are attracted to and following these new pioneers and leaders more than governments and corporations.

The steps to move to and through the Alchemy Prism to be part of this transformation cannot possibly be captured in the pages of this book. It is not that it can't be done—though few have the perseverance and focus to reach this level—it is that I am learning the climb myself today. You have just as much opportunity to move up to the Alchemy Prism as me! Because I can tell you what needs to be done: Once again, there are just three steps out from Blue Conductor to Indigo Trustee.

Three Steps From Blue to Indigo

Moving from Blue Conductor to Indigo Trustee, where you lose a part of your freedom as you become accountable to the cause that you represent, is a step that both Peter Diamandis and Richard Branson were moving to when I met them.

I first met Peter Diamandis when I traveled from Bali to the NASA center in Silicon Valley, where he had set up Singularity University with Ray Kurzweil. When I met Peter, he was already used to dealing in millions of dollars. He had set up the X Prize as a way to encourage space travel with a $10 million award to the first person to send a rocket into suborbital space and return safely.

He did this before he had the money; he was driven by a mission to push forward the frontiers of space travel. In the eleventh hour, he raised the $10 million from the Ansari family, and following Burt Rutan's winning flight, the X Prize became a driver for the future, incentivizing inventors to compete to solve our grand challenges. Using his Blaze Genius to connect with futurists, pioneers, and entrepreneurs, Peter has become a Trustee for our future, attracting the smartest minds and the deepest pockets in the industry.

A year later, thousands of miles away in the British Virgin Islands, I spent a week with Richard Branson on Necker Island. He talked about his own venture into space with Virgin Galactic and how he connected with Burt Rutan on his prizewinning flight, at the invitation of Peter Diamandis, to start his new space-traveling venture. Despite already being a billionaire, Richard has also been stepping into his role as an Indigo Trustee, being a role model for the world's entrepreneurs with his books, talks, videos, and blogs.

Now, many Blue Conductors choose to stay at Blue Level, which gives a life of luxury and wealth without the need to be accountable for the world's challenges. Increasingly, however, we are seeing Blue Conductors take responsibility for solving our grand challenges and moving to Trustee Level to lead. An Indigo Trustee makes the music possible, like a theater trustee who provides the name and resources for the composer and performers to make the music in the concert hall.

Here are the three steps that Peter and Richard took when they chose to move to Indigo Level:

1. **Trump Your Trust:** When you trump your trust, you use the trust you have built in your market to do more than simply create wealth. Peter used his trust in the space industry to bring together a panel of astronauts and members of NASA to launch the X Prize. Richard used his track record and reputation with Virgin Group to launch his books, sharing his message that anyone can start their own business and be a force for good.

2. **Capitalize Your Currency:** Blue Conductors have built assets that in themselves are tradable. Often these are the shares in your publicly traded business. Other times these are intangible assets like brands and reputation. Richard has used his businesses and Virgin brand to fund his contribution, for example, with his airline financing new green energy and environmental solutions. Peter capitalized on his reputation to launch the X Prize. When Google's Larry Page approached him, he launched a Google X Prize to land a vehicle on the moon. Since then, he has grown X Prize into a game changer, funding a string of innovation competitions that are solving major challenges in the world today from poverty to health care to preserving the environment.

3. **Connect Your Community:** When you see your market as a community, everyone is a customer, partner, participant, and advocate. Peter set up Singularity University to bring together a community of futurists and leaders collaborating for a brighter tomorrow. Richard set up Virgin Unite as his charity to connect social entrepreneurs and change makers around the world.

Why had I been investing time with Trustees like Richard and Peter? Because I had earned the right to be a Blue Conductor, but I didn't know these three steps to move up to Indigo Trustee. As a result, ten years ago I made some missteps attempting to move from Blue Level to Indigo.

Back then, I had a vision of "World Wide Wealth" where we could unite social entrepreneurs to create more and contribute more. I put my efforts and resources toward a network that grew and flourished but ultimately failed to sustain itself. I wasn't ready for the politics and conflicts within the community we grew. I wasn't prepared for the critics and growing pains that having a greater cause attracts. And I hadn't invested the necessary time to learn from Trustees who were forging their own journeys and had already weathered similar growing pains.

As at every level in the Wealth Lighthouse, it is a quantum leap to an entirely new experience at the next level. That's why I needed time with Trustees like Peter and Richard: to learn the language of the Indigo Level. Having learned from my failures and invested time to connect with and learn from those successful Trustees, I am on a renewed journey to shine a light on a cause: growing financial literacy for both our current and future generations.

For me to achieve my path, and for you to achieve yours, takes trust: a natural trust that links to our genius.

Trust in the Genius of Blue

To move from Blue Conductor to Indigo Trustee is to move from growing capital to mobilizing trust. In fact, most wealth creators at Indigo Level have trusts to own their assets. The trust you build in your market is linked to your industry and allows you to be a voice for change. But what we are trusted for varies according to our genius.

Dynamo Genius Is Trusted for Innovation

You tapped your creative spirit as a Dynamo Genius to move through the Foundation and Enterprise Prisms. Provided that you persevere, you will find in the future that the track record you build will earn you the right to become a Trustee of your cause in the future.

Dynamo Geniuses like Richard Branson or Bill Gates are trusted for their creativity. Each has used a pioneering spirit to create new markets and to think globally about solving big challenges. Through their ventures they have built a track record of innovation, so when Richard Branson says he is going up in space or Bill Gates says he will eradicate polio, people believe them.

Blaze Genius Is Trusted for Leadership

You will follow your Blaze path to success through your natural leadership skills. This will earn you the right to be a voice in your own community as you grow your connections, respect, and reputation. It's just a matter of time.

Blaze Geniuses like Peter Diamandis and Oprah Winfrey are trusted for their ability to bring the best people together. Both have used their ability to connect and bring out the best in people to grow their own influence and reputation. They have then leveraged this trust to move their communities, whether it is Oprah being a force for good through her Oprah's Angel Network or Peter pushing forward innovation with the X Prize and Singularity University.

Tempo Genius Is Trusted for Service

You followed your Tempo Genius path by taking care of the small things, building your track record as dependable and compassionate.

This will earn you the right through your actions in the future to speak with a trusted voice of authority on the cause you champion.

Tempo Geniuses like Mahatma Gandhi and Mother Teresa were trusted for their ability to serve. Both used their natural sensory acuity to be an advocate for change through compassion. Gandhi used his training as a lawyer to lead India to independence. Mother Teresa used her path as a missionary to help the poor in India. Neither needed to spend much time being creative or connecting with others as the quality of their words and work defined them. The care they showed in their day-to-day actions led to a level of trust in each of them that spread around the world.

Steel Genius Is Trusted for Reliability

You followed your Steel Genius by using your analytical skills and systematic thinking. This will earn you the right to propose bigger, more complex, world-changing missions in the future. Having the trust of others to deliver will give you the power to make a big difference in the world once you move to Indigo Level.

Steel Geniuses like Larry Page and Salman Khan are famous for their systems thinking and attention to detail. Each has built a track record for his ability to create complex global platforms that look simple, and both have used that trust to gain support for global projects to give rather than to get. Larry is collecting all the world's information online with Google. Salman is growing Khan Academy to provide education to students and adults around the world. Both are providing this knowledge for free to the public.

When you look at the inspiring leaders in the world, you will notice that many of them are not saying things or believing in a future that much different from what you may be saying or believing. The difference is that they have invested the time to earn the right to lead. They followed their genius path to the top of the lighthouse.

But they are still on the same path that you are. By seeing them as different from yourself, you give up hope that you could make the difference that they are making. By seeing them as simply being on a different step of the journey but using the same GPS, you can connect the dots and see that all that separates you from them are the steps in between. We may be different colors, but we're all part of the same rainbow.

The Alchemy Prism

To reach the top levels of the Wealth Lighthouse takes perseverance and commitment. Yet everyone who has reached the Alchemy Prism will tell you that it *wasn't* because of "me." They will tell you they are fortunate to be there, and they will credit a large part of their success to luck, saying something like *I was in the right place at the right time.*

The truth of it is, we create our own luck. When we set up a rhythm for our time and we open the space to get out of stress and into flow, we open up the space for magical time. When professional athletes feel this way, we say they are "in the zone." They are attracting the ball and scoring opportunities more often and are ready for those opportunities when they arrive.

How can we grow our own luck? A simple way to look at it is by breaking down luck into LUCK: Location, Understanding, Connections, and Knowledge.

LOCATION

In sports, knowing that the game is only on when you're on the field means showing up in the right place for the game. That includes setting up the space for your five energies and means showing up where the resources you need are in play. Every industry has a place where influencers and leaders connect with each other. If you're not in that place, you're not in the game.

UNDERSTANDING

Being on the field doesn't mean you end up scoring. Understanding you're there to kick the ball instead of watching the game changes your focus. It means you start looking out for the opportunities coming your way. You stop chasing the ball and begin positioning yourself based on where everyone else is and where you can be of most value. That's what it means to fill a gap in the market. Where you can be of most value to others is where the money will flow to you. This understanding changes your awareness of where flow is already occurring.

CONNECTIONS

You can be on the field, passing and ready to kick the ball. But if there are no team players on the field with you, you will be waiting a long time for that ball to come back. Connections are about knowing that flow grows the more you are connected to others playing the same game as you the right way. The more you share opportunities and resources with others, the more they will share them back (as long as they are the players on the field and not the spectators in the stands).

KNOWLEDGE

Even by being at the right place at the right time, with your team delivering you the ball, you still won't score if you don't know how to kick it. This doesn't happen by reading a book. It happens by practice: To know and not to do is not yet to know. Each level of the Wealth Lighthouse leads you to a higher level of competence in kicking the ball, until scoring comes naturally.

Having a rhythm every week that builds your Location, Understanding, Connections, and Knowledge builds your luck. It also builds your fortune. In fact, the word *fortune* comes from the

Roman goddess Fortuna, who is the guardian of luck. When we follow our flow, we find our fortune, which means three things:

1. **Luck:** To have good fortune is to have good luck. As your luck and synchronicities grow, you know you are on the right path.
2. **Wealth:** To have a fortune means to have financial wealth. If it feels like hard work, you're doing the wrong thing. Fortune doesn't come by holding on, but by letting go and following your flow.
3. **Legacy:** To be able to tell your fortune is to be able to see your future. As you follow your flow—and live your genius—you become clearer about your life purpose and the legacy you will leave.

To that end, in the Alchemy Prism, your genius becomes your legacy. Each of the four geniuses leaves a different legacy.

We all have greatness inside us and the potential to leave a legacy of our own. When we triangulate fortune and see our luck, our wealth, and our legacy linked to each other, we can spot the signs when we are moving toward and away from our flow. We can increase the magical moments in our lives and turn those magical moments into quantum leaps.

Three Steps From Indigo to Violet

We are now seeing a new group of change makers who have earned their way up the Wealth Lighthouse and are leaving their legacies. They are coming up with new ways to solve our big challenges. They are coming from a deeper level of understanding and have earned a greater degree of trust. Every one of us can rise to this level. Simply by taking one step at a time, you can step up to this level. Because even up here it is just about three steps.

Bill Gates is an example of someone who has moved from Trustee to Composer as a Dynamo Genius using these three steps to move from Indigo to Violet Level:

1. **Ratify Your Right:** You cannot nominate yourself to Violet Composer. It needs to be ratified by popular vote. This might be an actual formal vote, such as the presidential elections, or your community can recognize you as its leader. But it goes way beyond your business and its shareholders. By being invited by governments and institutions to support their efforts, Bill Gates, through his and his wife's foundation, was given the right to lead by those around him.

2. **Complete Your Composition:** All Composers are judged by the quality of their composition. This is more than a purpose in life: It is a deep understanding of the Composers who came before you, what they tried, how they succeeded, and how they failed. When Bill Gates turned his attention to education and global health, he became part of a line of Composers before and after him.

3. **Embrace Your Enemies:** Each of these levels takes you on a journey deeper at sea where the waves have higher highs and lower lows. As a Composer, you will have people who see you as their savior and people who see you as their enemy, which is why all Composers have bodyguards, as their greatest risk is the risk of losing their life. The president of the United States receives dozens of death threats every day. The third step at Composer Level is to be at peace with these lows as well as the highs at this level of presence.

Three Steps From Violet to Ultraviolet

While a Violet Composer makes the music, the Ultraviolet Legend is a symbol of our time. A legend on a map is the set of symbols that are used in place of words. When your mission becomes your life, and your life becomes a symbol for a generation, you reach Legend status.

Violet Composers do not take the three steps to Ultraviolet alone. They are lifted up the steps by the movement they have created:

1. **Personify Your Purpose:** Think of the people through history who are symbols of their time. Nelson Mandela made the stand against apartheid in South Africa and became the symbol of his cause.

2. **Surrender Your Self:** When we get into our flow, we lose ourselves in our work. When we fully surrender, we are willing to put our cause above our life. All Legends go through personal sacrifice for their cause. Legends are living missions that are all-consuming.

3. **Lose Your Life:** If you are going to reach the level of Legend, there is a good chance it will happen after you pass away. Many Composers become Legends only after they lose their life. However, there are living Legends who are already symbols of their time.

That last step is the reason Ultraviolet is the final—one might say ultimate—level of the Wealth Lighthouse. From Infrared to Ultraviolet, there are nine levels in all. These are the nine levels in which all humanity flows. We are all part of the same quantum leaps that make up light. Only when we divide it up can we see the steps and see that we are all part of the same rainbow.

Your Legacy

At the three levels in the Alchemy Prism, your Genius will shine through. The Trustees, Composers, and Legends of our time shine brightly through their Genius. At Alchemy Level, your Genius becomes your legacy.

Dynamo Geniuses Leave a Legacy in Their Creations

Dynamo Legends like Thomas Edison and Leonardo da Vinci have left a legacy in their creativity. The innovations we have today have come from a life of ideas that have given us new ways of doing things. As a Dynamo Genius, the innovations you leave can change the course of humanity.

Blaze Geniuses Leave a Legacy in Their Message

Blaze Legends like John Lennon and Martin Luther King Jr. have left a legacy through the power of their message. We have changed the way we think and what we are willing to believe and strive for as a result of their words. As a Blaze Genius, your message can shape a movement and lead to lasting change.

Tempo Geniuses Leave a Legacy in Their Actions

Tempo Legends like Nelson Mandela and Mother Teresa have left a legacy through the way they lived their values. We have changed the way we act and the values we live by through their example. As a Tempo Genius, your ability to live your truth through all adversity can shift the actions of a generation.

Steel Geniuses Leave a Legacy in Their Thinking

Steel Legends like Andrew Carnegie and Isaac Newton have left a legacy in their body of knowledge. We have changed the way we think and the theories by which we understand the world through their IDEAS. As a Steel Genius, the way you make sense of the world can lead to a shift in a nation's thinking.

On the Millionaire Master Plan, we use these Legends on the map to help us navigate our way. They are like landmarks orienting us on our journey—until we become landmarks and Legends ourselves.

ACTION POINT

The Eight Questions to Begin Every Day

Experiencing the magic of the Alchemy Prism does not need to begin sometime in the distant future. It can begin today. You are already the composer of your own life. Knowing you have the power to create your own music, how would you compose each day so that each day is a masterpiece?

I f you are beginning each morning without a routine that gets you set for the day, you are setting yourself up to fail. You may have a morning mantra, but mantras often lose their power over time as our mind switches off after hearing the same thing repeatedly. If you have an exercise routine or meditate, that is a good start. But while these activities may center you, as soon as you jump into your day's activities, the stress returns.

All the successful people I've met have routines and regular rhythms to start the day that keep them at a high level of excellence. I set my rhythm every day with eight questions. I have asked them for the last twenty years. They soothed me at my Infrared state of emergency and focused me as I moved up the lighthouse, opening me up to new possibilities. That's because my answers are often different every day.

My eight questions are divided like the three steps you take at each level in Wealth Lighthouse: Showing Up (being present to your current life), Stepping Up (taking the right steps right now), and Giving Back (passing on the flow, dancing with the universe, and experiencing the magic of every new day). Add them to your routine, and modify them to suit you as you get used to them.

Showing Up

WHAT AM I GRATEFUL FOR?

Usually my answer to this question does not surprise me: my family, my health, or something fabulous that just happened. Sometimes it is unexpected, though—what I learned from an argument the day before or a difficulty I am facing. Either way, starting with this gratitude washes away any negative energy in you.

WHO DO I LOVE?

This question can also have unpredictable answers. Often the faces I see are my family and friends, but sometimes I see the face of someone I am frustrated or unhappy with or I think is feeling negatively about me. This question showers love like rain onto your life and can clear many relationship issues so nothing is left to build up into negative feelings inside you.

WHY AM I SO HAPPY?

It's nice to ask this question when I have many reasons to be happy. It's most effective when I have problems and issues that are making me unhappy. It makes you accept that you *are* happy—and helps you find the happiness inside you—despite any unhappiness or stress on the outside.

Stepping Up

WHAT AM I MOST COMMITTED TO?

This question brings out my most important commitment in the day to come. It may be an action, a way to feel, or a person to connect to. Look back at the end of each day to see if you have achieved this one commitment. If you have, you will have had a good day. If you have not, recommit for the coming day.

HOW COMMITTED AM I?

If there is something I have put off for some time, this question makes me think about my level of commitment and perhaps change it. For example, at Infrared Level your commitment could be to "Measure My Money." If this keeps showing up for a few days and you keep increasing your commitment toward it, your unconscious mind will eventually push your conscious mind to find a way to actually do it.

Giving Back

WHAT IS MY INTENTION?

This question is about what I can give to my world today. I may answer something very general: *Smile* or *Be disciplined*. Or something specific: *Go for a run* or *Be on time*. Setting an intention gives each day a flavor different from the day before.

WHAT IS MY WISH?

This question is about what magic your world can give to you. The more my life is in flow, the more this question becomes my most magical. I have wished, *The person I need to help me with my accounts appears* and *A new business partner calls me* and *I will get the answer I've been looking for*, and then during the day received exactly that.

WHY AM I HERE?

The most important of all the questions, this one is about your higher purpose. My answer changes depending on whether I am thinking about this moment in time or being alive on this planet.

I have had people at every level say they can't afford to take time for themselves. I have told them that until they find the time, nothing will change. There is always a way, so find the time for you. Start by opening each day with these eight questions. See every day as a new beginning for your bright future and start it as one more step toward your future self, moving up the lighthouse. Your future self will thank you for it.

THE LIGHTHOUSE

I n 2010, we looked out of the highest window in the fort of Qait-bay over the Egyptian city of Alexandria.

I was telling my children the story of the Tabula Smaragdina (the Emerald Tablet of Hermes). Legend held that Hermes Trismegistus wrote it and Aristotle taught one of his students about the power of its words. That student was the son of the king of Macedon and grew up to be known as Alexander the Great, who supposedly found the original Emerald Tablet in Egypt.

The legend continues that after finding the tablet, Alexander had a dream telling him to visit a small island called Pharos on the Mediterranean shore of Egypt. He did and built the city of Alexandria on the bay surrounding the island, as home to the Emerald Tablet. Within a decade, Alexandria had become the meeting point for the Western world. It became the location for the Library of Alexandria, which housed the world's written scrolls, and the home of Cleopatra, the last of the ancient Egyptian pharaohs.

After Alexander died, the Lighthouse of Alexandria was built on the island of Pharos. The lighthouse was divided into three parts, reflecting the three parts of the Emerald Tablet. It became one of the Seven Wonders of the Ancient World, and was the second tallest structure in the world, after the Great Pyramids, for many centuries.

The fort my family stood in as I recounted this story had been built on the island of Pharos a thousand years ago after the Lighthouse of Alexandria fell.

Until it fell, the Lighthouse of Alexandria was seen as a symbol of humanity, a symbol of safety for those returning home, and a symbol of adventure for those setting sail toward the open sea. The Lighthouse of Alexandria, like the Emerald Tablet and like this book and the Wealth Lighthouse within it, held a secret—a secret hidden in plain sight.

The secret is us: *We* are the lighthouse. Within each of us lies the power of the entire universe, simply waiting to be unlocked. The secret is not within the levels of the lighthouse and the steps that take you to the top. The secret is that they all lead to the light. The purpose of any lighthouse is not to illuminate itself but to illuminate others. By lighting ourselves, we tap into this power to light up those around us.

So the secret is not in this book, but in what happens beyond this book when you connect to your genius, follow your flow, step up the lighthouse, and light up the world as you give back to it.

Remember, if you lose your way, you simply need to come back to this book. Come back to your personal page and see where you are, where you are going, and how to take the next step.

We are all on the same journey seeking a light to illuminate our way—without realizing that the light we are seeking is already within us. I wrote this book for you, and I wrote this book for me. For we are the same. We are also different. We are each a lighthouse on the same seashore.

Together, we can light up the world.

ACKNOWLEDGMENTS

This book wouldn't have been possible without the help of many extraordinary people. First, to my wife, Renate, and my three children, Kathleen, Theresa, and Luke—we began this journey together and still have so many magic moments ahead of us.

To my Mom, Jorva, my Dad, Neil, my sister, Elaine, and my brother, Martin, thank you for all the excitement, adventure, and laughter that got us to where we are today.

To my Entrepreneurs Institute superteam, Shah Hamzah, Penny Wee, Suraj Naik, and Sandra Morrell, you are awesome and make everything effortless. To Simone Holt and the Entrepreneur Resorts team, to Michelle Clarke and the Talent Dynamics team, to Joe Chapon, Bobbi DePorter, Heather Yelland, and the Green SuperCamp team, and to all our partners and affiliates, thank you for your ongoing support and energy. From John Abbott and our Australia team, to Mike Clarke and our England team, Tamami Ushiki and our Japan team, Paxton Hsu, Sheila Wang, and our Taiwan and China team, Bea Benkova, Jan Polak, and our Eastern Europe team, Chris and Janet Attwood and all our new partners in the United States, I am so thankful we're on this journey together. You are each creating ripples that keep growing day by day.

This book is made up of so many stories, and I thank everyone I have featured for letting me be a part of your journey, and now for sharing that journey with a wider audience. A big thanks to my agent, Wendy Keller, for believing in me enough to take on this project, and to my co-writer and editor, Jim Eber. Thank you to my publisher and Rick Wolff for taking on the book, and to the team at Hachette, including Dan Berkowitz, Yasmin Mathew, Amanda Pritzker, and Tracy Brickman, and to Brigid Pearson for the brilliant cover design.

Thank you to my mentors, who have had such an impact on my own path: to Michael Braunstein, who first opened my eyes to what was possible, and to Goh Kim Siew, Richard Tan, Patrick Liew, Mike Harris, Paul Dunn, Jack Canfield, Richard Branson, Peter Diamandis, John Hardy, and Cynthia Hardy for guiding me and inspiring me through the standards you set in your own lives.

And finally, thank you, the reader, for picking up and reading this book, and for being on the same path that I am on—of ongoing self-discovery and self-mastery, to be the best lighthouse that we can be.

ABOUT THE AUTHOR

Born in Hong Kong and educated at Trinity College, Cambridge University, Roger became an entrepreneur before leaving college. He estimates the cost of his entrepreneur education was far greater than his academic education, losing many millions through his failures before achieving success. Today he owns and runs businesses in publishing, property, event management, resort management, training, coaching, mentoring, and online education.

Behind all of Roger James Hamilton's companies and content is his mission of "World Wide Wealth"—the power to grow our flow individually and collectively. Roger believes we each have the power to develop our own financial literacy to grow our own wealth, from which we then have the power to help those around us.

As a member of the Clinton Global Initiative, United Nations Global Compact, and Transformational Leadership Council, Roger has been dedicated to the global growth of Social Entrepreneurship for the last decade. He is also an Executive Graduate of Singularity University, based at the NASA Research Center in Silicon Valley. He conducts "Fast Forward Your Business" tours each year in Australia, Japan, China, Africa, England, and the United States on the Top 10 Trends impacting business, equipping entrepreneurs with the tools and future presence to navigate through the changes taking place in our economies.

Roger is the Founder of Entrepreneurs Institute and creator of the Wealth Dynamics & Talent Dynamics profiling systems used by more than 150,000 entrepreneurs and leaders around the world.

Roger's resort in Bali, Vision Villas, is Asia's first Entrepreneur Resort, running iLab accelerator programs throughout the year. These are one-month programs to help business owners transform their business into remotely operated, multi-market, multi-language global businesses.

Roger lives in Bali with his wife, Renate, and three children, Kathleen, Theresa, and Luke.

You can connect with Roger at www.rogerjameshamilton.com.

INDEX

BUSINESS PLUS

Recognized as one of the world's most prestigious business imprints, Business Plus specializes in publishing books that are on the cutting edge. Like you, to be successful we always strive to be ahead of the curve.

Business Plus titles encompass a wide range of books and interests—including important business management works, state-of-the-art personal financial advice, noteworthy narrative accounts, the latest in sales and marketing advice, individualized career guidance, and autobiographies of the key business leaders of our time.

Our philosophy is that business is truly global in every way, and that today's business reader is looking for books that are both entertaining and educational. To find out more about what we're publishing, please check out the Business Plus blog at:

www.businessplusbooks.com